Information Propagation on the Web 2.0

MARKETING IM GLOBALEN WETTBEWERB
MARKETING & GLOBAL COMPETITION

Herausgegeben von Oliver P. Heil

Vol. 2

PETER LANG

Frankfurt am Main · Berlin · Bern · Bruxelles · New York · Oxford · Wien

Mark Elsner

INFORMATION PROPAGATION
ON THE WEB 2.0

Two Essays on the Propagation
of User-Generated Content and How
It Is Affected by Social Networks

PETER LANG
Internationaler Verlag der Wissenschaften

Bibliographic Information published by the Deutsche Nationalbibliothek
The Deutsche Nationalbibliothek lists this publication in the Deutsche Nationalbibliografie; detailed bibliographic data is available in the internet at http://dnb.d-nb.de.

Zugl.: Mainz, Univ., Diss., 2010

Cover and Photo Design:
© Olaf Gloeckler, Atelier Platen, Friedberg

D 77
ISSN 1867-8424
ISBN 978-3-631-61747-2

© Peter Lang GmbH
Internationaler Verlag der Wissenschaften
Frankfurt am Main 2012
All rights reserved.

All parts of this publication are protected by copyright. Any utilisation outside the strict limits of the copyright law, without the permission of the publisher, is forbidden and liable to prosecution. This applies in particular to reproductions, translations, microfilming, and storage and processing in electronic retrieval systems.

www.peterlang.de

Preface

The diffusion of the Internet has considerably changed the basic principles of information exchange and, with it, the practice of Marketing. This new structure is now enabling user-driven conversations across most markets that were simply not possible in the previous era of unidirectional mass communication. In a matter of only a few years these processes have enabled the phenomenon of User-generated Content to develop into highly influential sources in the formation of public opinion about a wide variety of topics. Nowadays, every third Internet user is considered an active user in terms of writing blogposts or commenting on them, uploading Youtube videos, sharing photos on Flickr, or participating in social communities like Facebook or Xing.

As a matter of course, this implies a gaining importance of Social Media for the Marketing discipline. On the one hand, managers face a rapidly increasing amount of daily-published information targeting their companies and products that may develop to reach a wide audience, for better or worse. On the other hand, these new phenomena offer possibilities to interact with customers or other individuals in entirely new ways.

Various examples show that UGC has the potential to seriously affect firms within a couple of days or in hours, as the bicycle accessory manufacturer Kryptonite experienced. A cyclist figured out how to hack with just a ballpoint pen the $50 *Evolution U-Lock* that Kryptonite claimed to offer "toughest bicycle protection in moderate to high crime areas." The cyclist posted a video of the hacking trick on BikeForums.net. While the story was spreading fast from one website to another with more than 300,000 people having read just the two most popular posts in a few days (Polgreen 2004), Kryptonite chose to remain silent, in spite of being repeatedly contacted (O'Brien 2004). Finally, after a total of five days since the initial post, the story made the *New York Times* (with the headline "The story that infuriates bicyclists"). It was only then the firm responded with a lock-exchange program. Altogether this incident cost the firm more than $16 million and a considerable amount in damage to reputation and brand equity (Horowitz 2005).

Although this is a somewhat unusual example, it demonstrates one important marketing aspect of the power of UGC—the high degree of public and consumer scrutiny that can quickly emerge on the Web 2.0. Additionally, it is important to note that the rapidly developing and intense public attention generated on the Internet can significantly increase the newsworthiness of a story to mass media like the New York Times. This in turn can aid in further propagation of the information. Product malfunctions like the one described above often prompt individual consumers to share the information with a personal network of individuals. However, the Internet has completely changed the nature of such networks to one of social networks with far and wide reach by including large numbers of people who do not know each other personally. As a consequence, the scope, scale and speed of spreading the information have taken on an entirely different meaning and dimension on the Internet in general, and on the Web 2.0 in particular. Thus, firms can ill afford to take a wait and see attitude when a story about their product evolves.

The work described in this dissertation was carried out at University of Mainz and University of Colorado between January 2008 and December 2010. I am indebted to several people for the successful completion of this work. I am grateful for the generous support of my doctoral advisor Professor Dr. Oliver P. Heil. He has encouraged my research continuously and in many different ways and offered me opportunities to present my work in front of international audiences, allowing me to get unique and very helpful insights. It was this exposure that lead to an invitation by Professor Dipankar Chakravarti to visit Leeds School of Business, University of Colorado at Boulder, where I had the chance to spend eight months as a visiting research scholar. I am very thankful for this unique opportunity and the scholarship that was made possible by Professor Heil.

In my time at CU Boulder I had the chance to closely work with Professor Atanu R. Sinha. All the guidance and support he offered during my time there and afterwards were of greatest help and are truly appreciated. My thanks also go to the Wharton Interactive Media Initiative and Marketing Science Institute for financially supporting my research. Further, I thank my colleagues at Johannes Gutenberg University. In particular, Dorothea Rector and Sergio Moccia helped and supported me in many ways, creating a nice and pleasant working atmosphere.

Further, I owe a lot to my family, in particular my parents and my sister. I am truly grateful for their enduring and wholehearted support. And finally, my greatest thanks go to Katrin. She could not have been more supportive and caring throughout those years.

Mark Elsner

Table of Content

List of Figures 9
List of Tables 11

Essay 1: Spreading the Word 15
1. Introduction 17
2. User-generated Content and the Web 2.0 21
    2.1 Relevance 21
    2.2 Definition 23
3. Relevant concepts and literature 25
    3.1 Marketing relevance 25
    3.2 Motivation to participate 26
    3.3 Opinion Leadership 27
4. Conceptual Framework and Hypotheses 29
    4.1 Conceptual Framework 29
    4.2 Hypotheses 30
        4.2.1 Size of the submitter network 30
        4.2.2 Structure of submitter networks 32
        4.2.3 Cascades 35
5. Source network and data 39
    5.1 Source network structure 39
    5.2 The data 41
6. Findings 43
    6.1 Descriptive results 43
        6.1.1 Dynamics of overall voting pattern 43
        6.1.2 Distribution of popular stories 46
        6.1.3 Categorical analysis 47
        6.1.4 Network size and structure 48
    6.2 Empirical model and results 52
        6.2.1 Survival analysis 52

	6.2.2 Model specifications	53
	6.2.3 Model results for network size and structure	54
	6.2.4 Model results for user activity	59
	6.2.5 Model results for content analysis	66
6.3	Results for global cascades	77
6.4	Network analysis	81
7.	Conclusions	85
7.1	Discussion of results	85
7.2	Limitations and future research	86

Essay 2: How Social Netowrks Develop on the Web 2.0		89
1.	Introduction	91
2.	Utility of networks	93
3.	Development of egocentric network	97
3.1	General network formation	97
3.2	Initial stage	98
3.3	Tie strength	99
4.	Conclusion	101
References		103
Appendices		107
	Appendix 1: Data collection and transformation	107
	Data transformation	112
	Appendix 2: Additional figures and tables	113

List of Figures

Figure 1: Timeline of propagation for a randomly chosen set of popular stories (12 days) 44

Figure 2: Timeline of propagation for a randomly chosen set of popular stories (40 hours) 45

Figure 3: Time till popularity for 846 stories submitted Sept 14–20, 2009 46

Figure 4: Number of diggs in the 24h after submission 51

Figure 5: Subnetwork A 83

Figure 6: Subnetwork B 84

Figure 7: Number of popular stories per user. 113

Figure 8: Scree plot 125

List of Tables

Table 1: Distribution of users and their submitted front page stories 47
Table 2: Category * Status Crosstabulation 48
Table 3: Summary statistics for data period Sept 14-20, 2009 49
Table 4: Network size and activity 50
Table 5: Results for models 1a – 3a 55
Table 6: Results for model 1b – 3b 56
Table 7: Results for model 4 -6 58
Table 8: Results for models 10a - 12a 61
Table 9: Results for models 10b – 12b 62
Table 10: Results for models 19a – 21a 64
Table 11: Results for model 19b – 21b 65
Table 12: Results for models 25a – 27a 68
Table 13: Results for models 25b – 27b 69
Table 14: Results for models 28a – 30a 71
Table 15: Results for models 28b – 30b 72
Table 16: Descriptive statistics for Constructs 1 - 9 74
Table 17: Results for models 31a – 33a 75
Table 18: Results for models 31b – 33b 76
Table 19: Results of models 34 - 36 79
Table 20: Results for models 37 - 39 80
Table 21: Network statistics for subnetworks A and B 82
Table 22: Game 1 94
Table 23: Game 2 94
Table 24: Results of models 7a – 9a 114
Table 25: Results of models 7b – 9b 115
Table 26: Results of models 13a – 15a 116
Table 27: Results of models 13b – 15b 117
Table 28: Results of models 16a – 18a 118
Table 29: Results of models 16b – 18b 119
Table 30: LIWC 2007 Categories 120
Table 31: Eigenvalues and rotation sums of squared loadings 123
Table 32: Factor loadings and Cronbachs Alpha for new constructs 126
Table 33: Results of models 40 - 42 131

Essay I: Spreading the Word – Assessing the Factors that Determine the Popularity of User-generated Content

Abstract

In a matter of only a few years the diffusion of the Internet and the rise of Web 2.0 related technologies have enabled the phenomenon of User-generated Content (UGC) to develop into highly influential sources in the formation of public opinion about a wide variety of topics. However, little knowledge exists about the processes and factors that confer a given UGC a prominent level of attention. Such knowledge appears especially important since the vast majority of UGC dissolve almost unnoticed. This dissertation builds on the theory of Opinion Leadership and Homophily and focuses on the social network of a submitter to explain the process of propagation of UGC. I posit that it is the size and structure of the submitter's network that plays the crucial role in influencing whether or not certain content achieves a prominent level. In addition, I provide evidence that message-related factors seem of only marginal importance, at least until the respective content exceeds a threshold of public attention. Thus, I conclude that a new form of opinion leadership arises, derived mainly from the social location the submitter occupies. Further, I provide insights into how such networks develop. Overall, this research contributes towards the general understanding of UGC and information propagation on the Web 2.0. The dissertation provides insights into if and how individuals' unique social positions determine the propagation of information and promote certain content to reach prominence. Generally, I provide evidence that Internet-based networks may not work as effectively as has been often argued.

1. Introduction

One of the major research challenges faced in general when looking at UGC derives from one of the key aspects of UGC—it's sheer abundance. Each minute, thousands of weblog posts and comments are created and video clips and pictures are uploaded[1]. The vast majority of this content ends up insignificant and irrelevant to public opinion, or unobserved by many people but some of the content targeting products, companies, industries or governments—for better or for worse—indeed become popular.

Thus, the targeted entities need to pay close attention to this process of information propagation on the Web 2.0. In particular, it is crucial to understand what drives some content to reach prominence while others pass by unnoticed. Identifying such drivers make it easier for firms to monitor content in a systematic manner rather than spend lots of resources on monitoring all content. Yet, marketing and communication research has not quite addressed why and through what mechanisms the aforementioned process occurs. Thus, one of the most important research questions related to UGC refers to the processes and factors that confer certain content a high level of visibility, while others dissolve without attaining any significant public notice.

One widely used explanation refers to the often espoused concept of "the wisdom of crowds" which suggests that information aggregation from many individuals produces superior outcome than information from one individual (Surowiecki 2004 popularizes this concept in a book with the same title). In the context of Web 2.0, the concept implies that the new technical structures—or communication platforms—provided through the Internet enable individuals to combine and generate superior knowledge on *aggregate*. For example the broadly followed *Cluetrain Manifesto*[2] states in thesis "nine" and thesis "ten", that "[t]hese networked conversations are enabling powerful new forms of social organization and knowledge exchange [...] As a result, markets are getting smarter, more informed, more organized".

---

1 According to Google, in May 2008 there were about 10 hours of video uploaded to youtube every minute and those numbers increased by more than 60% in just 3 months. To illustrate: Hollywood would have to produce about 55,000 movies a week to amount for the same quantity of material. Other numbers suggest that around 1,000,000 blogposts are created every 24h, not counting the comments on the posts.

2 The Cluetrain Manifesto (www.cluetrain.com) is a set of 95 theses published in 1999. The 95 theses address the impact of the Internet on consumers and organizations within the newly connected marketplace of the Internet

Along these lines, it can be argued that groups of loosely organized individuals manage to filter out information that provides the highest utility at the macro level. If each user assessing a piece of information applies his/her individual evaluation criteria of news value, at the end the information with the biggest intersection of value perceptions should emerge—which would imply a high quality of the content.

While in theory these arguments have appeal, it is an open empirical question whether in practice, as seen on the Web 2.0, there is evidence to support generation of superior information based on the "wisdom of crowds"[3].

In this research, as detailed later, I expect other factors to be at work in the propagation of information that conflict with the concept of the "wisdom of the crowds". A more specific research question relates to the role some individuals play in the process of information propagation—or in other words—how personal influence within a social network takes on a major role in the propagation process.

As "the social interactions that develop around the content are the key to understanding the importance of [...] user-generated content" (Cooke and Buckley 2008, p. 274), I focus on the social position users occupy within social networks to explain how UGC gains popularity. I posit that the probability of specific content achieving a high degree of popularity is mainly determined by the social location the author/submitter (one who submits a story to the website), and/or the promoter (one who endorses/votes on the story) occupies within a relevant social circle.

Quite naturally, it is to be expected that aspects of the message itself, like message factors and the type of content, may explain the spread and prominence of specific UGC. However, in this essay I focus on the role of submitter's egocentric social networks in the process of information dissemination beyond that of the message aspects. Counter-intuitively, it is suggested that the message aspects are of secondary importance in most situations relative to the network based factors.

---

[3] The latter presupposes that benefits from information aggregation occur to the extent evaluation by users / contributors are independent of one another. However, if the independence starts to weaken or breaks down then aggregation may not necessarily lead to superior information since some / much of the information become correlated.

Section 2 of this essay addresses the relevant concepts and literature. I first discuss the concepts of Web 2.0 and User-generated Content, before focusing on Opinion Leadership and finally analyzing related marketing literature. In section 3 I develop the framework and posit the hypotheses.

Section 4 describes the source of data and the data retrieval approach. Section 5 states the findings of the empirical analyses. In section 6 I address limitations of this work and conclude.

2. User-generated Content and the Web 2.0

2.1 Relevance

There is growing agreement among researchers and practitioners about an ongoing media revolution. For decades mass media were dominated by the publisher/editor on the one side, pre-defining through selecting and editing content what was consumed on the other side by the numerous recipients. Today we are experiencing user-driven technologies that allow content to be increasingly "pulled" by users, rather than "pushed" onto them.

Over the last few years the Internet has undergone fundamental changes towards user-driven technologies, like blogs, social communities and video-sharing platforms, to name a few. Collectively, these technologies have enabled a revolution in terms of users generating and posting content on the Internet. The results of which are referred to as User-generated Content. This has lead to truly global and interactive communities and a ubiquity of user opinions about a multitude of issues.

At the same time these consumers of content also publish or submit content themselves accounting for the interactive structure of the Web 2.0 that is increasingly influencing public opinion. Along with the seemingly fading distinctions between publisher and recipient, the boundaries separating professional and amateur publishers are vanishing. Or, in other words, the consumer now plays a really central role in the formation of opinion about companies and products as well as a variety of other issues.

The outcomes of this development are felt all-around us, even by those that are not highly involved with this "social revolution" (Smith 2009):

1) Related closely to marketing is the fact that the results of a search for product information are dominated by other users' opinions and remarks. The online reviews and star ratings found at many e-retailing sites, like Amazon, are only one of many examples.
2) Additionally, egocentric networks[4] are becoming more and more influenced by digital spaces like Facebook or the social news site Digg, such that individuals are exposed to the opinions of "strangers" to a greater extent.

---

4 Defined as the individual and his immediate friends, i.e. looking at a network from the perspective of one node.

3) Even those that are not actively participating in anything related to the Web 2.0 are influenced by this development as User-generated Content is increasingly affecting traditional media as the introductory example has shown.

In 2006 the Time Magazine chose "You" as the person of the year and stated in the cover story (Time Magazine 2006):

> "It's a story about community and collaboration on a scale never seen before. It's about the cosmic compendium of knowledge Wikipedia and the million-channel people's network YouTube and the online metropolis MySpace. It's about the many wresting power from the few and helping one another for nothing and how that will not only change the world, but also change the way the world changes".

By choosing "You" as the person of the year, the editors of Time Magazine paid tribute to the millions of internet users dedicating their time and creative energy to the booming next generation of the Internet. The cover story heralded all the users producing the so-called User-generated Content (UGC). "After decades of vilifying the passive couch potato, the press now venerates the active participant in digital culture" (van Dijck 2009, p. 41). Only two months earlier, the UGC-platform YouTube had been acquired by Google in a spectacular deal for 1.65 Billion US$ (Sorkin 2006).

Both incidents represent a significant step in the evolution of UGC:

1) The broad recognition as a powerful new information channel, and
2) The enormous economic value that is often attributed to UGC.

Another aspect underlining the relevance of UGC is the fact that in 2006, user-generated content sites, platforms for photo sharing, video sharing and blogging, comprised five out of the top 10 fastest growing U.S. Web brands (Nielsen 2006)

2.2 Definition

The rise of UGC was ultimately enabled through the development that turned the Internet into the so-called Web 2.0[5]. Building on new technologies the Internet evolved into a participative web, allowing for interaction, like blogging, commenting or voting. Even though in my understanding the most important facet of the concept Web 2.0 is referring to a paradigm change in communication, it is through new web services and web based applications that users are able to collaborate (OECD 2007). The notion of "Web 2.0" was developed in a brainstorm meeting in 2004 between Tim O'Reilly and Dale Dougherty and introduced to the public during the "Web 2.0 Conference" in San Francisco in the same year. Following Musser and O'Reilly (2006, p.4) the concept can be defined as follows: "Web 2.0 is a set of economic, social, and technology trends that collectively form the basis for the next generation of the Internet—a more mature, distinctive medium characterized by user participation, openness, and network effects."

Because the definition remains somewhat imprecise and lacks concreteness the concept of Web 2.0 has often been labeled a "catch phrase" or "buzzword" that was created after the burst of the dot-com bubble to capture the dynamic potential of the Internet after many had lost hope in it (e.g. Pisani 2006, Shannon 2006). However, even if not precisely defined, certain broad elements exist that facilitate the understanding of this concept. Following Pisani (2006) these are:

1. Platform: The Web is the platform through which almost everything can be done.

2. Receive/publish/modify: This platform, amongst other things, allows for interaction. Once information is discovered or received it can instantly be published and conversations may begin. Through comments and the possibility to upload and link additional content, the original piece of information itself changes.

3. Broadband: Throughout the world connection speeds and flatrates are on the rise, enabling users to share text, pictures and videos easily and at marginal costs close to zero.

---

[5] However, the concept of Web 2.0, or participative web as it is sometimes referred to, is a broader phenomenon than just UGC. The respective web technologies allow for interaction on many different dimensions (thus determining the Web 2.0) are also used by commercial ventures.

4. Contributions: The capacity enhancing broadband aspect facilitates users' willingness to share what they have with others.

5. Network effects: Multiple contributions are supposed to create a sum of knowledge greater than its parts. This changes the nature of knowledge, suggesting the potential to harness collective intelligence.

3. Relevant concepts and literature

3.1 Marketing relevance

The outcomes of different elements of the Web 2.0 have been the focus of marketing research recently. In this work, mainly the influence of online product reviews and other forms of online conversations on product choice or adoption is observed (e.g. Chevalier and Mayzlin 2006; Godes and Mayzlin 2004; Huang 2006; Mayzlin 2006; Senecal and Nantel 2004).

As an emerging insight, one could argue that online messages, mostly created by amateur users, have a significant influence on consumers, even if such reviews have occasionally been proven to be manipulated (Kornish 2009). This goes along with the traditional findings that word of mouth (WOM) represents an important source in opinion formation. For example, Chevalier and Mayzlin (2006) observe the effect of consumer reviews at online bookstores on relative sales. Those reviews include so-called *star ratings* as well as additional written comments. The authors find evidence, that the relatively rare negative one-star ratings carry a lot more weight than the positive five-star ratings do, which is consistent with prior research on WOM (e.g. Arndt 1967). In respect to the additional written comments Chevalier and Mayzlin (2006) find that the "results on the length of reviews suggest that consumers actually read and respond to written reviews, not merely the average star ranking summary provided by the Web sites", implying that information processing occurs beyond the superficial level. This insight has important implications for managers considering the opportunities and potential threats of UGC. Negative content on the Web 2.0, tackling firms or products, is shown to have a higher impact while spreading faster and wider.

The context of this dissertation is distinct from the previous research which emphasizes the utility of UGC (such as product reviews) for consumers' purchase decision making and for firms' marketing decisions. In this research, the focus is decidedly on information generation and propagation aspects of UGC that do not necessarily have direct and immediate utilitarian value to the user, nor does it have measurable utilitarian value to the user. For example, consider the social news sites on the Web 2.0. The UGC on these sites purportedly inform the readers on a variety of issues and creates a forum for information exchange on the issues. A reader does not necessarily rely on the gained knowledge, if any, to inform a decision (such as choice of a product). The benefit a reader may accrue from the information exchange could derive from being a part of the formation of public opinion and / or being part of influencing a public agenda. In this sense the value is more hedonic in nature than utilitarian. As a consequence, the processing of UGC and the drivers of popularity of UGC in my context are likely to be very different from those examined in the context of product choice.

Studying UGC in the context of this dissertation is a very important step toward understanding the fundamental functioning of formation of opinion on the Internet. In particular, the basic question is whether or not such formation of opinion and influences reflect *objective* information aggregation based on message factors and type of content as indicated in 'the wisdom of the crowd' or suggested in the *Cluetrain Manifesto*? Or, does the information aggregation suffer from *subjectivities* not germane to the content and message factors of the information? Such subjectivities, if present, ought to make us wary of the efficacy of information dissemination via this medium. This issue is relevant to policy makers and businesses alike since the Internet based social news sites are becoming increasingly popular and displacing the traditional news media as harbinger of information on topics from business, to entertainment, to politics. The paucity of academic research focusing on these issues makes the current effort worthwhile to pursue.

3.2 Motivation to participate

While UGC is growing both in quantity and impact, less is known about contributors' motivation to participate. However, this motivation is critical for UGC in general. This is because content is provided, assessed, promoted and commented on largely by volunteers who put in significant amounts of time and effort in return for no monetary and other obvious rewards. Therefore, the question about what motivates contributors and which motivations are associated with higher and lower levels of contribution is a central one (see Nov 2007 for a similar argumentation).

In terms of volunteering behavior, six motivational categories or drivers can be identified (Clary et. al 1998, Nov 2007):
1. Values: Altruistic and humanitarian concerns can be expressed through volunteering. Contributing to UGC sites actively shows that concern by sharing knowledge and spreading what they consider as worth sharing.
2. Social: Volunteering can provide individuals the chance to be with others and to engage in activities viewed favorably by relevant others. This is particularly true for UGC.

3. Understanding: Through volunteering, people may have the opportunity to learn new things and to exercise old knowledge, skills and abilities.
4. Career: Job-related benefits can be obtained by volunteering. This could relate to the preparation for a new job or the maintaining of relevant skills.
5. Protective: This refers to the protection of the ego from negative features of the self.
6. Enhancement: Somewhat related to the former category, enhancement involves protective strivings of the ego rather than the elimination of negative factors.

3.3 Opinion Leadership

In the research on formation of public opinion the work on the *two-step flow of communication* represents a milestone. Formulated by Katz, Lazarsfeld et al. in the 1940s and 50s, the theory proposes that a small minority of *opinion leaders* act as intermediaries between the mass media and the majority of society (Katz and Lazarsfeld 1955). This group of Influentials[6]—as they are sometimes referred to—actively consumes, interprets and passes on media content to the lower end media users, thus inheriting a central role in the formation of public opinion. In the years following this work, the theory has developed into a central paradigm for research on the propagation of information in sociology and marketing as well as in communications research. This holds true even though the concept itself has undergone some changes (see Watts and Dodds 2007 for a comprehensive overview).

Originally, opinion leadership was conceptualized as a combination of personal and social factors. According to Katz (1957) those are: (1) the personification of certain values ('who one is'), (2) competence ('what one knows'), and (3) the strategic social location ('whom one knows'). Thus, to be an opinion leader it is "not enough to be a person whom others want to emulate or to be competent. One must also be accessible". Persons combining these factors—the opinion leaders—are defined as "individuals who were likely to influence other persons in their immediate environment" (Katz and Lazarsfeld 1955, p. 3).

However, following this conceptualization, opinion leaders are not persons that stick out of the crowd in a traditional sense, such as celebrities. Rather, their in-

---

[6] Another related concept refers to "Market Mavens" (Feik and Price 1987). Even if there are conceptual differences the main idea behind Opinion Leaders, Market Mavens and Influentials remains the same: Certain individuals influence the information others receive and the way the recipients process it.

fluence derives from their informal status as individuals who are highly respected, informed or simply connected fairly well (Watts and Dodds 2007). The structure of communication has significantly changed since the days Katz and Lazarsfeld published their work as Watts and Dodds (2007) have argued. That is, we moved from the two-step flow that has dominated decades of mass-media towards a multistep flow of communication. Typically, there is no longer one individual picking up and processing the information for his opinion followers. Instead, the roles of Opinion Leaders may be varying and even though the definition may hold true for one person in one context, the situation might be different if the topic changes.

4. Conceptual Framework and Hypotheses

4.1 Conceptual Framework

This research focuses on the question how and why certain UGC gain a high degree of popularity. To be precise, I mainly analyze the processes and factors that lead to a certain degree of visibility, i.e. where the respective content exceeds a well-accepted threshold and is exposed to a public audience that is fundamentally greater than the network of the submitter. The definition of this threshold in general is somewhat arbitrary. However, below I motivate and specify my definition of this level more precisely.

To further address the general research question, the empirical part of this dissertation focuses on the social news site Digg (www.digg.com) that appears to be a good representation of the Web 2.0 and UGC-related processes for the following reasons. Digg, and social news sites in general, act as information filters or aggregators that—through the participation of users—extract certain content out of the abundance of all UGCs and thus "grant" it prominence or popularity (hereafter, I use the word 'popularity'). Importantly, these sites operate without editors and completely rely on the participation of users. That is, users are self-organizing through these sites. As the 'About Us'-section of Digg states: "we're here to provide a place where people can collectively determine the value of content". Thus, such structures are representing what has been described as "participatory democracy" (Fuchs 2007).

In the case of information dissemination, this process confers to each user— apart from the right to submit whatever content he considers worthy—the same right as everyone else to promote content submitted by others.[7] On social news sites the process is operationalized as follows. A registered user *submits* content (e.g. a blogpost, video or picture) to the social news site. I refer to this user as the *submitter*. Subsequently, the content appears on the site and other users can *view* this content and possibly *promote* it by voting on it—a common practice in Web 2.0-related environments. The action of promoting—or in more general and technical terms (referring to the practices on the Web 2.0 in general) linking to the original source in order to spread the news—instead of replicating it, is a cornerstone of UGC and the Web 2.0.[8] I refer to a user promoting content as the

---

[7] Or in other words: "One Person, One Vote".
[8] The well-known blog search engine Technorati, for example, establishes it's ranking of the top-blogs on the number of incoming links from other sites. The common method of linkbacks is a toolset for web authors to obtain notification who linked to their articles.

promoter. Thus, the process of spreading UGC involves two basic steps: First, the submitter generates content and submits it and second, other users read (*view*) and may promote it. Importantly, subsequent manipulations of the original content (e.g. the post, the video, etc.) are not possible, although promoters may *comment* on stories—a widely observed practice in Web 2.0 related environments.

To recap, I distinguish between the four basic actions of *submitting, viewing, promoting* and *commenting* on content. For completeness, I add that each registered user can execute each of the identified actions. Furthermore, the users of social news sites form networks—another cornerstone of the Web 2.0. Network members are usually informed about the actions of other users who belong to their network. Hence, the process of information dissemination on social news sites starts with the submission of a story[9]. Subsequently, if activated, other users view the story and promote it. An important question is whether and how membership in a network of the submitter impacts promotion of a story. If the membership matters, whether its influence is of primary or secondary importance relative to the message factors and the type of content associated with the story. In the following I argue that the social location of the submitter and the network characteristics are of primary importance in the propagation of UGC.

4.2 Hypotheses

4.2.1 Size of the submitter network

Earlier I have mentioned three characteristics of Opinion Leaders: (1) personification of values, (2) competence and (3) strategic social location (Katz 1957). In the context of Internet-based UGC, the third characteristic is becoming more crucial for the following reasons. Naturally, the personification of values as well as the competence is much harder to assess in an UGC environment, where most users hardly know about one another. Message boards, weblogs, social news sites and other platforms enabling the publishing of UGC are vastly characterized by anonymity. In most cases only a cryptic screen name is displayed. Therefore, "[u]ltimately, our identities as well as incentives are obscure in the virtual world" (Mayzlin 2006, p. 155).[10]

---

9 In the following we use story, content and UGC synonymously
10 This anonymity, for example, allows firms to easily disguise promotional activities as UGC.

However, information about the strategic social location is usually at hand. As this information consists of publicly available numbers referring to the size of the user's network, it stands to reason that the size of the network also contributes towards the social status of a user within the network. In the social news sites where personal information is reduced to sparse user profiles, no hierarchies exists and no other form of differentiation is readily identifiable. Thus, it is the number of persons belonging to a submitter's network that mainly provides differentiation. This becomes more compelling if one recalls that relationships on social news sites are mostly casual since these individuals know very little about one another except their counterparts' usernames. In this context it is useful to highlight some major conceptual differences between social news sites and social networking sites, like MySpace, Facebook or the Korean site Cyworld, of which the latter has recently been analyzed by Goldenberg et al. (2009):

1) The main purpose of social news sites is to submit and spread information of which the submitter and promoter(s) assume that they contain a certain degree of news value and thus provide valuable insights for the readers. The main purpose of social networking sites on the other hand is to share information about the users' lives and connect with friends (which of course does not exclude that news stories are posted).

2) The above highlighted difference leads to two different types of user profiles themselves. While the profiles on social news sites usually provide very limited information about the individual behind it—apart from screen name and information about the corresponding network—the user profile itself is the major component on social networking sites. The context of focus here is social news sites.

This property of social news sites makes the size of a user's network particularly relevant for the investigation of popularity of UGC.

In this context it is of importance to contrast social networks with groups of individuals. "Groups are simply defined by membership based on one or more actor attributes […] without taking into consideration the pattern or structure of ties" (Van den Bulte and Wuyts 2007, p. 14). Applied to my unit of analysis, this means that all registered users of a social news site form the group of users while at the same time social networks among these users exist. The users and their relationships represent the pillars of a social network respectively labeled as nodes and links (connecting ties between users).

I view the propagation process of UGC—and to be more precise, the promotion until a threshold of popularity is achieved—mainly as a flow of information through such a social network. Thus, the strategic social location—or in other words the size of the network—should fundamentally determine the role of opinion leaders and their success in submitting content that will later become popular. This is of particular importance in the case of UGC, as here social ties can be achieved more easily, implying that a highly connected individual can instantly reach hundreds or thousands of other users via the Internet. As a result, I hypothesize:

> **H1a**: As a submitter's network size increases, the likelihood of reaching a threshold of popularity increases-- irrespective of content and message factors.

Similarly, if a user has practically no network, no other user will be informed about his activity. Even though a submitted story will appear besides all the other stories—just like a story submitted by a user with a large network—I assume that there is only a small, random chance that this story will be read and promoted by other users. Thus, I assume that a story has no chance of getting popular if no user with a considerable network submits it.

> **H1b**: If a submitter has no network or a network of insignificant size, content submitted by this user is unlikely to reach the popularity threshold.

4.2.2 Structure of submitter networks

So far I have discussed the aspect of network size and the resulting strategic social location and how I assume that it contributes towards opinion leadership. Additionally, a central strategic location empowers what Bikhchandani et al. (1992) call one of the most striking regularities of human society: "localized conformity", also referred to as "homophily" (Lazarfeld and Merton 1954), meaning that individuals who are similar tend to associate with one another and act alike.

At many different UGC-related sites two basic types—or directions—of relationship can be identified, if observed from the perspective of a singular user (for reasons of clarity subsequently defined as user A):

> 1) The users that choose to befriend A usually do so by clicking on a button and without approval of A are instantly informed about the activities of A, i.e. what he or she submits or promotes.

2) User A himself is informed about all the actions of the other users that he *chooses* to befriend. Relationship can also be reciprocal or mutual, such that two users, A and B, both get informed about what the other one does.

Focusing on user A and considering his stories' likelihood to become popular, I only need to observe a unidirectional flow of information (which is information flowing from A to all the users that are listening to him). However, the strength of relationships among different users in a network is not the same and could differentially impact the promotion mechanism at work. In particular, two classes of users are identified based loosely on the concept of strong and weak ties.

At first sight, this structure relates to the concept of the "strength of weak ties" postulated by Granovetter (1973). This somewhat counterintuitive concept implies that even though individuals know their strong ties better and have more intense interactions, the weak ties are more important for the diffusion of information. This is because the individuals a person has strong ties with, all tend to know each other well. As a consequence, they tend to share the same limited information and are less likely to offer new information. Weak ties, on the other hand, do not tend to know each other well and are more likely to introduce new information. Importantly, the theory is less about the strength of ties itself but about the bridging function that weak ties imply, as they "provide people with access to information and resources beyond those available in their own social circle" (Granovetter 1982, p. 113). However, I do not assume that the pattern under observation follows this theory. On the one hand, following Granovetter's definition, social ties in the internet should in general be rather "weak". On the other hand, I primarily focus on the first steps of information propagation and do not explain the entire process of information diffusion.

In the following, I label the strong and weak ties respectively as *friends* and *fans* and define as follows.

If B befriends A the former is informed about the actions of the latter, but not vice versa, I call B a *fan* of A.

If A now chooses to befriend B the relationship becomes two-sided and I define B as a *friend* of A. Therefore my definition of friendship always implies mutuality.[11]

---

[11] For completeness I note that for the focus I take in this article the relationship would not be considered at all if A were a fan of B, as B would not be informed about any of A's actions and the relationship could not affect A's stories' likelihood to become popular.

Having defined two categories of relationships within a network, I build on the theory of homophily, mentioned earlier. Homophily refers to the fact that a contact between similar people occurs at a higher rate than among dissimilar people or in other words that "similarity breeds connection" (McPherson et al. 2001, p. 415). No matter what type of information flowing through networks, it tends to be "localized", implying that distance in terms of social characteristics relates to network distance—or the number of relationships through which a piece of information must travel to connect two individuals. This results in more homogeneous networks with regards to many different characteristics that limit peoples' social worlds in a way that has powerful implications for information exchange and attitude formation. However, it is not only that similar people tend to group together and that interaction leads to shared knowledge but also that these similar people then tend to interact, thus that relative shared knowledge leads to interaction (Carley 1991, McPherson et al. 2001).

Based on the concept of homophily, I argue that individuals that are more alike tend to form closer relations as well as being supportive of the same information. Applying this to the network structure offered above, this implies that *friends* are more closely connected than *fans* as the former group's degree of similarity and interactions are supposedly higher—or to be precise, that interaction is only possible if users are *friends*. By contrast, fandom refers to a unidirectional relationship where only one looks at the actions of the other and thus structurally prohibits interaction. Also, in practice, the numbers of a user's fans may reach the tens of thousands, as detailed later, a fact that prohibits individual interaction anyway.

Hence, I hypothesize that for a story to get popular, the submitter's *friends* are more important than the user's *fans*[12]. This is somewhat counterintuitive from the perspective of Granovetter's theory of the strength of weak ties (1973). Further I note that, from the technical operation aspect of the sites, friends and fans are treated in an identical manner when it comes to transmission of information. Both receive information about the submitter's action in the same way and the reciprocity of the relationship for one group (friends) does not confer any advantage on this information transmission.

I assume that the submitter's friends are more influential than the fans:

> **H2**: For a story to reach threshold of popularity, the submitter's friends are more influential than the submitter's fans, irrespective of content and message factors.

---

12 Of course this implies that the respective users need to have both friends and fans

Furthermore, considering the egocentric network of user A, it is reasonable to argue that his friends may receive an additional value if they belong to a proportionately small and thus exclusive group, rather than belonging to a proportionately large group. For example, consider networks of users A and B. User A has 50 friends out of his network size of 5,000 (i.e., remaining 4,500 are fans), while user B has 50 friends out of his network size of 200 (150 fans).

The friends of A feel a more exclusive relationship when they find how selective A has been in befriending them (only 1% have been befriended). On the other hand, friends of B feel less exclusive in their relationship since B has befriended 25% of the network members. Since in networks on social news sites, for the most part, there is no relationship preceding the network (that is, no personal connection between members beyond this network) and there is no other association of exclusiveness available to the friends beyond this proportion. The more exclusive friends—as judged by this proportion (smaller proportion)—will tend to promote more due to their stronger sense of connectedness to the submitter, relative to less exclusive fans (larger proportion). Put differently, the effect of the submitter's friends on the likelihood of a story reaching a threshold of popularity is moderated by the size of the fans' circle. This leads to:

> **H3**: The influence of submitter's friends is moderated by the number of his fans (such that the smaller the proportion of friends, the stronger their influence of causing a story to become popular).

4.2.3 Cascades

Information dissemination on social news sites starts with the submission of content by an actor. Subsequently, other actors may view the content and may promote it, resulting in a sequence of actions—that is, activations by actors—referred to as a "cascade" (Watts and Dodds 2007). After "all" actions have occurred, the size of the cascade can be judged by cumulating the number of activations. Cascades can be of any size. Watts and Dodds (2007) categorize cascades into two types: "local" and "global" cascades. "Local cascades affect only a relatively small number of individuals and typically terminate within one or two steps of the initiator. (...) Global cascades are the opposite—they affect many individuals, propagate for many steps, and are ultimately constrained only by the size of the population through which they pass. Importantly, global cascades can only occur when the influence network exhibits a 'critical mass' of early adopters" (Watts and Dodds 2007 p. 445).

This structure finds a natural translation to the information propagation context of social news sites. After a story is submitted and until it reaches the prominent/popular status (that is, the story appears on the front page(s) on the site), the visibility of the story to the population of social news site users is limited. Efficacy of search suggests that users are more likely to view stories that appear on the front page(s) rather than look for stories that are deep down which would require higher level of effort and time. Such search efficacy emphasizes the need for stories to achieve popular status in order to have wider visibility. Following Watts and Dodds (2007) I posit that popular status is achieved through a "critical mass" of early backers. Moreover, consistent with Watts and Dodds (2007), I identify the *local cascade* as the phase from submission until the popular status is reached, and the *global cascade* as the phase which begins once the popular status is achieved. Given cascades can be of any size, not every local cascade reaches the critical mass necessary to start the global cascade, nor each global cascade becomes big. For the purposes at hand, I rely on the characteristic that a critical mass on the local cascade is necessary for the global cascade to begin.

Thus far, my conceptual development of UGC-related information propagation (in sections 2.1-2.2) has been confined to the phase of a local cascade. I have argued in Hypotheses 1-3 that the network characteristics play a crucial role, irrespective of message factors, in propelling stories to a prominent/popular status (that is, appearance on the front page(s)).

A follow up question that arises is what happens when the story reaches the popular status beyond broadening the *potential visibility* of the story and starting a global cascade? What process of information propagation takes place in this phase of a global cascade? These questions merit attention since it is the size of the global cascade—when the story becomes visible to the entire population of users—which signals the *actual* interest level of the population of users and determines which stories have the highest appeal. Intuitively, one might argue that in the global cascade phase the major influence for propagation comes from non-network users since (a) they easily become aware of a story *only* during this phase (by contrast, users who are part of the submitter's network are notified of a submission and thus become aware in the local cascade phase) and (b) they are collectively much larger in size than the size of the submitter's network (a submitter's network is likely to be a relatively minor subset of the set of all users). This line of thinking suggests the following:

The actors within the egocentric network of the submitter are likely to have an insignificant effect on information propagation during the global cascade phase. I have argued earlier in sections 2.1-2.2 that actors in the submitter's egocentric network are responsible for the popularity in the local cascade phase. Such an egocentric network evolves around a few individuals and thus is unlikely to represent the interests of the universe of non-network users.

Additionally, the very act of joining such an egocentric network suggests a desire for *belonging to a group* among these actors and a motivation to promote the group's activity. This sets apart the motivation of actors belonging to a submitter's network from those individuals in the much larger universe of non-network users. Following these arguments I suggest that since in the local cascade phase the likelihood of popularity is driven positively by actors in the submitter's network, once the story begins the global cascade these very actors are likely to have a negative influence on the information propagation. In summary, I forward a counterintuitive thesis that in the global cascade phase the characteristics of the submitter's network will likely have a negative influence on the information propagation—rather than the intuitive thesis of no significant influence. Thus,

> **H4**: Conditional on a story reaching the global cascade phase, the larger the share of the submitter's network promoting the story in the local cascade, the lower the likelihood of the story becoming a success in the global cascade phase.

5. Source network and data

5.1 Source network structure

To test the hypotheses I use data from the leading social news site Digg (www.digg.com). Digg is arguably the most important and largest SNS occupying rank 100 among the most popular websites worldwide. As a comparison, the website of CNN is ranked 65, The New York Times 101, The Huffington Post 174 and the Wall Street Journal 290. Also, its popularity is global in scope as shown in the rankings for the following selected nations (ranks in parenthesis): Pakistan (18), India (32), United States (43), Canada (50), Indonesia (51), South Africa (55) and Australia (57) (Alexa 2010). At Digg information dissemination basically follows the patterns described in section 2^{13}. The actors could be classified into three categories:

(i) members of the submitter's network,

(ii) registered users who are not members of the submitter's network

(iii) non-registered users.

Actors in category (i) can be either *friends* or *fans*. The categories (ii) and (iii) are together classified as non-network users. The category (i) users get notice of submission ("push" information).— Members of the categories (ii) and (iii), namely, non-network users, receive no such notice of submission; however they can go to the site and check for stories ("pull" information). Efficacy of search suggests that members of categories (ii) and (iii) are more likely to review stories that appear on the front page(s) rather than look for stories that are deep down in the upcoming section, which would require higher level of effort and time.

Such search efficacy emphasizes the need for stories to reach the front page for those to have wider visibility. Furthermore, members of categories (i) and (ii) can *view* a story, and/or *vote* on a story, and/or *comment* on a story. Members of category (iii) can only *view* a story. Given this structure of Digg, members of category (i) have earlier and more opportunity (only this category among the three receive "push" information and have superior privileges of view/vote/comment) to aid the story to reach the front page in the local cascade phase. A registered user can upload an unlimited number of stories, videos or

---

13 Note that Digg references stories from other online sources, as it is usually the practice on social news sites. Apart from the headline (which is also the link to the source) only three lines of text describing the referenced story are displayed. This is edited by the submitter.

images given that they do not violate Digg's terms of use. More precisely, the user links to the respective content (news article, video or image) that is available from other sites. He then chooses a title for the submission (max. 60 characters) as well as a short description (max. 350 characters) that label his submission. Additionally the user needs to specify a category under which the content appears. Digg automatically fills in these fields with the title of the referenced web page and the introductory text/the first lines of the article, if existent. It is common practice for most users to use this text or alter (shorten) it only marginally.

After a duplicity check the content appears in the upcoming section, where all submitted contents appear in chronological order. Each content—indentified through the URL—is allowed to be submitted only once. However, the duplicity check also checks for stories that may be of the same or similar content and the user is then asked to assess the question of duplicity. This seems to be accomplished mainly through keyword comparisons. After that the submitter is presented with a list of potential stories he is supposed to check for duplicity and subsequently asked to confirm that his story has no duplicates that have already been submitted by clicking on the appropriate button. After completing the submission process the story appears in the upcoming section of the site (in reverse chronological order of time of submission) where it can be viewed by everyone accessing this section of the site. Additionally, members of category (i) get informed about this submission (under "friends' activity"). Users that belong to (i) and (ii) can also vote and comment on the story.

If and when the story is promoted to the front page (that is, becomes popular), a global cascade is triggered. Very importantly, the algorithm which determines popular status is not publicly disclosed by the operators of Digg, who justify this secrecy based on concerns about manipulation. What is observable though is the variance in the number of votes (hereafter, referred as *diggs* to be consistent with the Digg nomenclature) it took for a story to move to the front page, as well as the time a story took to reach the front page. Also, the network size and structure in terms of friends and fans can be observed at Digg.[14]

---

14 However, even though Digg uses the same terminology my definition of friends and fans offered above shows some structural differences. Digg defines friends as all the users the submitters befriended (including the one-sided) while fans are those who befriended the submitter. In my definition friends are those with two-sided relationship with the submitter, and fans are those who befriend the submitter without the later reciprocating. Notably (and different from my usage) mutuality cannot be addressed in this structure of Digg.

5.2 The data

I collected several datasets from Digg. Details of the data collection process and of the data organization appropriate for analysis is available in Appendix 1.

First I take a macro view of the information propagation on this site. Thus, stories which appear on the front page, i.e. become popular, are reviewed. A sample of 111,484 front page stories submitted over a 3 year period (October 2006 till September 2009) is gathered and analyzed to understand the variation in number of popular stories by submitters. I call this dataset 1.

Then I collect data, namely dataset 2, to address the major thesis in this essay: What drives a story to the front page? This second dataset consists of all 117,624 stories submitted by 38,546 unique users to Digg over 1 week between September 14, 2009 00:00h GMT and September 20, 2009 23:59 GMT. The data include time of submission, time of reaching front page (promotion to popular status), the content category (entertainment, gaming, lifestyle, offbeat, science, sports, technology, or world and business; as classified by Digg), media type (text, image, or video), submitter's user name, information on the actions of digging (i.e., voting) and commenting and the network information for each submitter.

Additionally, in order to track the continuing lifecycle of the stories submitted in this 1 week period, beyond this week, data on diggs and comments and views are collected for 12 days after the last story was submitted. The data for this additional 12 day period also allows me to track the rate of success of stories in the global cascade. While the choice of 12 days may appear somewhat arbitrary at first reading, I justify this by noting that all important processes in information propagation have occurred by then and only few stories experience a slight linear growth of votes.

The respective stories make it to the "top" section of the site, where the most dugg stories in 24h, 7, 30 and 365 days are displayed. To illustrate: A story about Michael Jackson's death, submitted on June 25th 2009, had gained a total of 25,012 diggs by Jan 7th 2010.

At this point of time only one story was slightly ahead (25,734 diggs) reporting that Barak Obama officially becomes the 44th American President. Naturally this story was submitted about five months before the other one. 24 hours after the submission of the Michael Jackson story it had already gained 22,560 diggs (or 90% of the total number at Jan 7th), after 4 days 23,800 users (95.2%) had voted for the story and in the 100 days before Jan 7th (94 days after submission) a total of only 383 users (0.015%) have added their vote[15]. Note that the story made it into the "top" category in less than 24 hours and has remained there since then.

In order to account for *history* of submitters' activities and other users' actions on submissions, a third dataset is collected and consists of the 4 weeks preceding dataset 2. This third set contains data from August 17, 2009 00:00h GMT till September 14, 200923:59h GMT and produces information on additional 445,314 stories submitted by 96,845 unique users.

Several steps were necessary to transform the raw data to a point that allows for the analyses I present in the following. These steps are described in Appendix 1.

---

15 It is interesting to note that it is generally reported that the original source for the death report was TMZ.com, where a short article was posted at 21:20 GMT. At 21:43 the story I describe here, referencing the TMZ.com post, was submitted to Digg and promoted at 22:11. However, the first mention of Michael Jackson's cardiac arrest was submitted at 20:51 (promoted at 21:50). In between these two stories, 27 other stories had been submitted to Digg reporting about the cardiac arrest, including several that reported the death.

6. Findings

6.1 Descriptive results

6.1.1 Dynamics of overall voting pattern

An observation of the development of diggs over time has revealed highly dynamic patterns of information propagation (see Figure 1 and 2 for a randomly chosen set of popular stories). A typical story accumulates diggs rather slowly within the first hours after being submitted. After getting promoted to the front page an evident increase in the digging frequency occurs. Once a story reaches the front page, a global cascade (as defined in section 3.3) is initialized. The initial global cascade phase basically determines the number of diggs a story will eventually gain, before another evident change in digging frequency occurs—this time a sudden drop. The diggs gained after this drop—which for most stories occurs after two to four days—acumulate to a very small and insignificant share of the number of total diggs.

The diggs gained after this drop accumulate to a very small and insignificant share of the number of total diggs (compare the Michael Jackson example cited in section 5.2).

An analysis of the time it took all the popular stories in the sample to reach the front page unveiled the following results. The minimum time was 1,217 seconds (or 20.3 minutes). The maximum time was 169,835 seconds (or 47.18 hours). From the frequency chart in Figure 3 it is apparent that there is a concentration towards the first half of the time span. After 24h 93.1% of the stories had reached front page, after 13h, two thirds had made this transition. Every fourth story reached status popular in less than 4 hours.

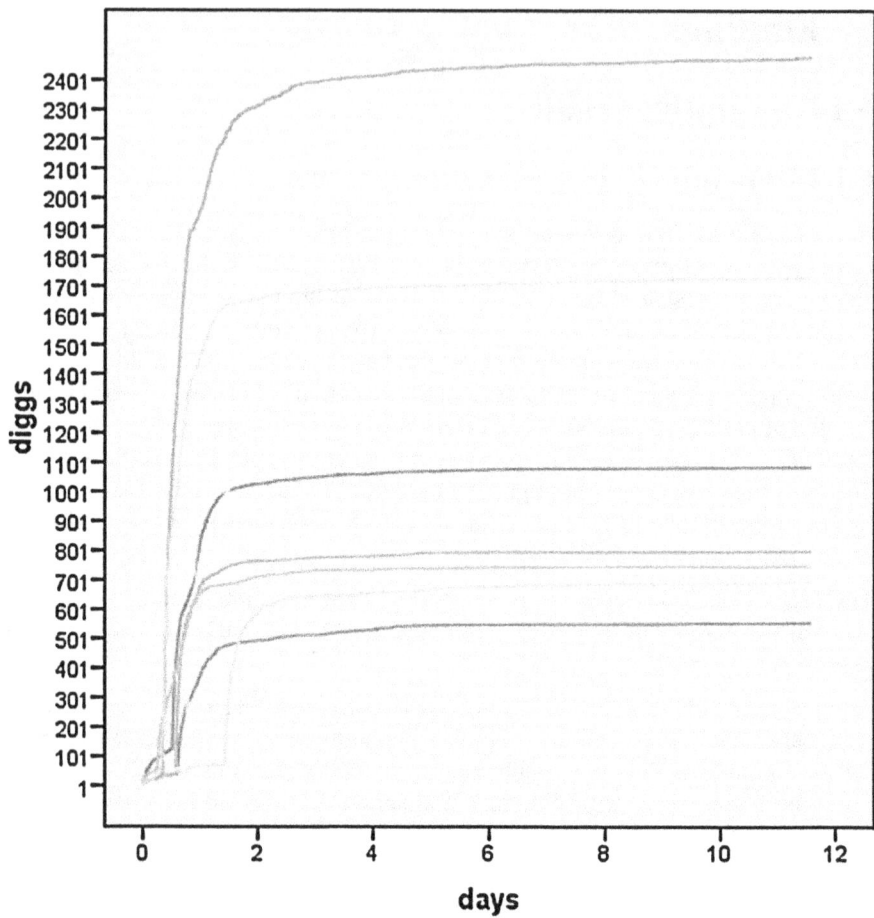

Figure 1: Timeline of propagation for a randomly chosen set of popular stories (12 days)

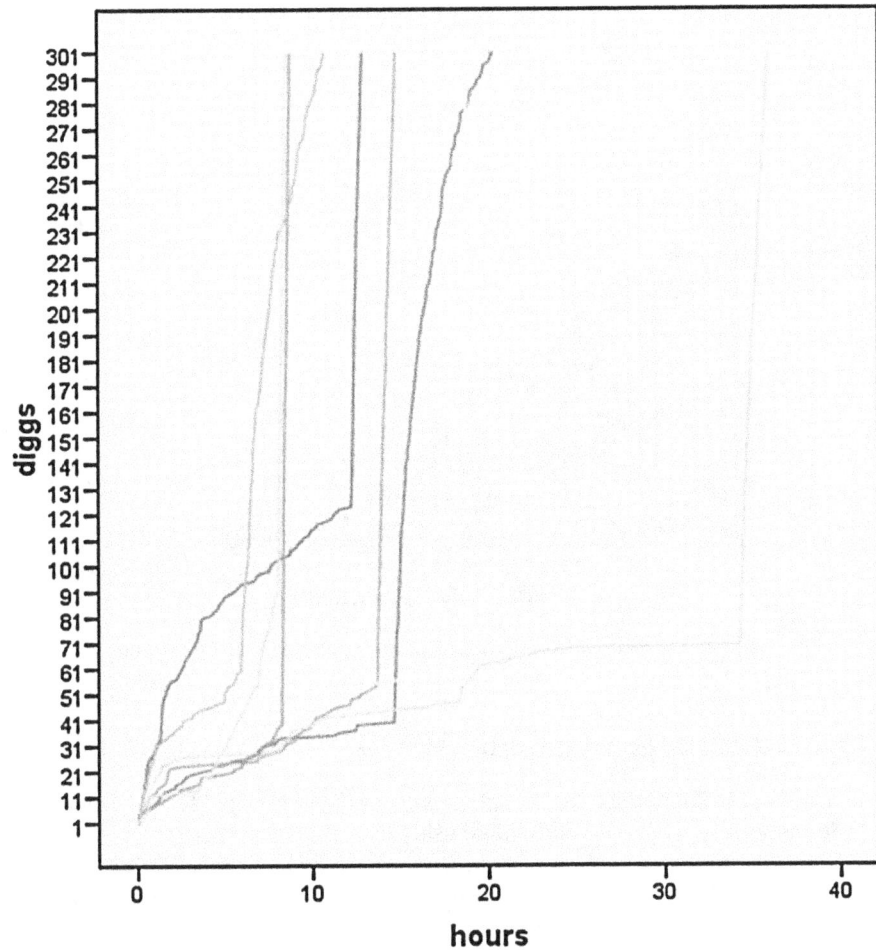

Figure 2: Timeline of propagation for a randomly chosen set of popular stories (40 hours)

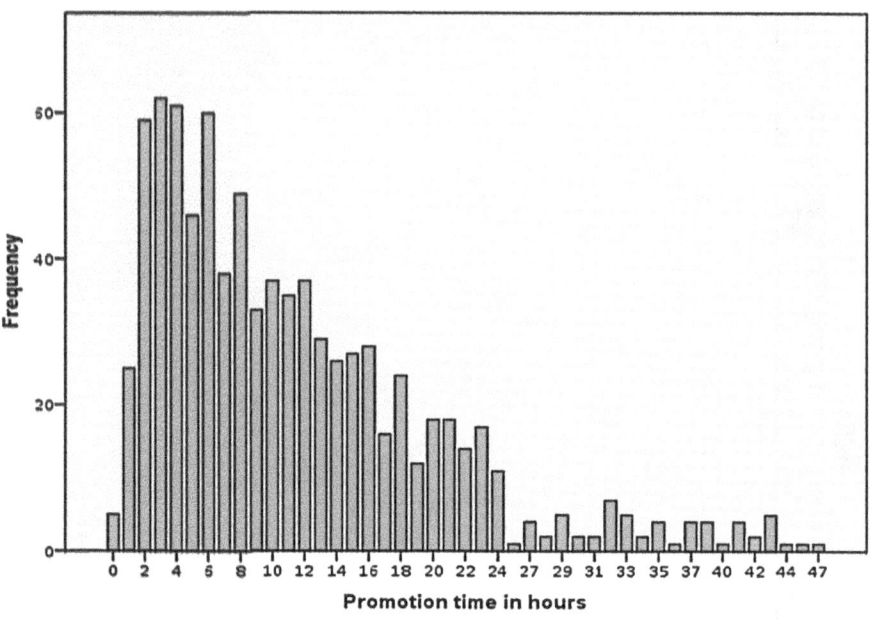

Figure 3: Time till popularity for 846 stories submitted Sept 14–20, 2009

6.1.2 Distribution of popular stories

Next, I discuss some descriptive statistics from dataset 1 on 111,484 front page stories submitted by 20,595 individual users over the 3 year period. The focus of this analysis lies on the number of stories submitted by each user, given that the user submitted at least one story during the course of the three years that later became popular. It is really striking to see the highly skewed distribution of success (defined as number of popular stories) within this group of 20,595 submitters[16] (see Table 1; Figure 7, Appendix 2).

The most successful submitter, namely "Mr.BabyMan", managed to submit 3,617 stories that later became popular. Over the course of three years he thus had on average 3.3 stories per day on the front page. However, there are other highly successful submitters, such that the six most successful users submitted 10% of the front page content, 24 users submitted 20% and 212 users (or 1% of

---

16 Note that all of these 20,595 submitters have already achieved the success of submitting at least one story that made the front page.

all the successful submitters) were responsible for every second story on the front page.

On the other hand I observed 14,091 submitters that got only one story to the front page. This implies that 68.5% of the submitters of popular content were responsible for only 12.5% of the front page content.

Table 1: Distribution of users and their submitted front page stories

No. of users	% of users	Share of popular stories
Top 1	0.00005 %	3.2 % (3,617 stories)
Top 6	0.0003 %	10 %
Top 24	0.0012 %	20 %
Top 212	1.03 %	50 %
14,091	68.5 %	12.5 %

Figure 7 (Appendix 2) represents the heavily skewed distribution even within the top 1% of the successful submitters. Again, it is important to highlight that at this point I only analyze the submitters of popular stories, or in other words, stories that trigger a global cascade. I address what happens to these popular stories during the global cascade phase in a later subsection.

These results already strongly indicate that certain users are more influential than others and that "opinion leaders" seem to exist in propagating a story to the front page in the local cascade.

6.1.3 Categorical analysis

As mentioned above, the submitter needs to specify a category under which he wants the submitted content to appear. More precisely, he chooses a subcategory which is assigned to one of the eight main categories. These main categories are (subcategories in parentheses):

Technology (Apple, Design, Gadgets, Hardware, Industry News, Linux/Unix, Microsoft, Mods, Programming, Security, Software),

World & Business (Business & Finance, World News, Political News, Political Opinion),

Science (Environment, General Sciences, Space),

Gaming (Industry News, PC Games, Playable Web Games, Nintendo, PlayStation, Xbox),

Lifestyle (Arts & Culture, Autos, Educational, Food & Drink, Health, Travel & Places),

Entertainment (Celebrity, Movies, Music, Television, Comics & Animation),

Sports (Baseball, Basketball, Extreme, Football - US/Canada, Golf, Hockey, Motorsport, Olympics, Soccer, Tennis, Other Sports),

Offbeat (Comedy, Odd Stuff, People, Pets & Animals).

The frequency of the chosen categories varies greatly.

Table 2: Category * Status Crosstabulation

		Status		total
		popular	upcoming	
Category:	Entertainment	107	18,279	18386
	Gaming	38	4,784	4,822
	Lifestyle	134	26,814	26,948
	Offbeat	132	10,798	10,930
	Science	122	3,542	3,664
	Sports	52	7,518	7,570
	Technology	151	18,069	18,220
	World & Business	110	26,974	27,084
Total		846	116,778	117,624

6.1.4 Network size and structure

My basic thesis for information propagation in the local cascade phase rests on properties of the submitters' network. To shed light on the hypotheses H1-H3, I use dataset 2 which comprises data on all stories submitted during a randomly chosen 1 week period—start of September 14, 2009 to end of September 20 2009—as described in section 3.2. During this week's period the total of

117,624 stories were submitted by 38,546 distinct users. Of these, 846 stories got promoted to the front page (submitted by 290 users), resulting in a 0.71% hit rate (846 out of 117,624) and a user success rate of .75% (290 out of 38,546). The total number of diggs for all stories amounts to 927,836 (as of October 2, 2009), resulting in an average of 7.89 diggs per story (see Table 3).

Table 3: Summary statistics for data period Sept 14-20, 2009

No. of submitted stories	117,624
No. of popular stories	846
Avg. no. of diggs for all stories (local cascade stage)	7.89
Avg. no. of diggs for popular stories (local cascade stage)	89.11
Avg. no. of diggs for popular stories (global cascade stage)	683.04

Next, I offer several descriptive results based on these 117,624 stories (see Table 4). Although at the aggregate level, the statistics nevertheless reveal some intriguing insights. Comparing the subset of popular stories versus the set of all stories, the means of friends and fans are roughly ten and forty times larger, respectively (13.10 vs. 141.53 for friends and 68.49 vs. 2787.27 for fans). An important implication is that the networks of submitters whose story become popular are much larger in size than networks of all submitters, suggesting a probable role of networks in making a story popular.

For the local cascade phase considering all stories, the digging activity is characterized by friends voting on more stories compared to fans (7,535 vs. 4,631 stories) plus friends voting about 2.5 times as much per story (mean of 13.34 vs. 5.55 diggs – see Table 4). For the subset of popular stories, friends vote four times as much as fans per story in the local cascade stage (39.89 vs. 9.69), but friends vote only 1.4 times as much as fans in the global cascade phase. These aggregate findings indicate a probable stronger role of friends relative to fans in the propagation process in the local cascade. This effect is more notable because there are fewer friends than fans on average in the networks (13.10 vs. 68.49 – see Table 4).

Table 4: Network size and activity

All stories No. of Submitters = 38,546	No. of stories	Individual Measures		
		Max	Mean	SD
Friend network for submitter		860	13.10	50.988
Fan network for submitter		15,561	68.49	584.899
Friends voting at local cascade stage	7,535	110	13.34	21.223
Fans voting at local cascade stage	4,631	41	5.55	6.574
Popular stories No. of submitters = 290				
Friend network for submitter		632	141.53	91.694
Fan network for submitter		15,561	2787.27	2836.834
Friends Digging at local cascade stage	815	110	39.89	21.213
Fans voting at local cascade stage	780	41	9.62	6.892
Friends voting at global cascade stage	798	79	16.04	12.450
Fans voting at global cascade stage	794	145	11.46	11.704

A visual representation of the average number of friends and fans digging in the upcoming stage is shown in Figure 4. The results are displayed in hourly segments and focus on the first 24h after submission only. Note that the bars for friends and fans are a subset of the total number of diggs. The left y-axis indicates the number of diggs while the right y-axis shows the scale for the number of remaining upcoming stories at the respective hour (indicated as triangles).

In order to check for the role of network size, a look at submitters with no network reveals that while 53,757 stories out of 117,624 (45.70%) are submitted by users with 0 friends and fans, only four stories submitted by users with 0 network made it to the popular status (0.47%), supporting H1b.

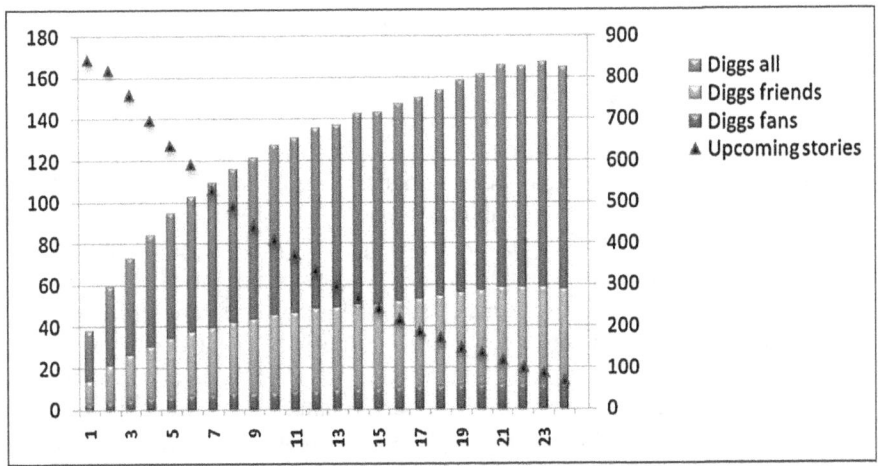

Figure 4: Number of diggs in the 24h after submission

To examine the role of the number of submissions by users, I compare the hit rates of the top ten submitters of *popular* stories to those of the top ten submitters of *all* stories during that week (both defined as the ten users submitting the most stories in the respective categories). The first group submitted a total 187 stories of which 115 eventually became popular, accounting for an average hit rate of .615 (range .31 to .92). The top ten submitters for all stories submitted a total of 2030 stories of which only 2 made the front page, leading to an average hit rate of .000985. The two most active users in this group submitted 360 stories each during the course of one week without getting a single story to the front page. These findings suggest that likelihood of a story reaching the front page is not driven by the frequency of submission.

In summary, based on the descriptive statistics presented thus far, among other things, I find preliminary evidence that a relatively small group which is part of the submitters' network has disproportionate influence on making a story popular with friends having more impact than fans, and that the size of network matters.

6.2 Empirical model and results

6.2.1 Survival analysis

Regression models are widely used in empirical research. They are applied when the influence of independent predictor variables on the magnitude (or at all occurrence in logistic regression) of an observed dependent variable is the focus of analysis. The analysis of *survival times* is a special type of regression analysis that does not only consider whether an event occurs or not but also how long it takes till the event occurs. The focus of survival analysis is on a group of individuals for each of whom or which there is a defined event occurring after a length of time. Such events are often referred to as *failures* or *hazards* even though the event occurring can also be a performance. Such data exist in many forms and a multitude of disciplines such as clinical studies, reliability analyses in engineering and recently also studies in econometrics and physics (Kalbfleisch and Prentice 2002). To determine failures and failure times precisely, three requirements have to be met (Cox und Oakes 1984):

1) The time origin must be precisely defined for each individual. However, it does not need to be (and in most cases is not) at the same calendar time for each individual.
2) A time scale for measuring failure time must be defined. This is usually real time, although other possibilities exist, like operating time of a system, mileage of a car or measures of cumulative load encountered.
3) The meaning of failure must be entirely clear. In medical studies this could be death or death from a specific cause—which naturally leaves little arbitrariness in the definition. However other settings exist, where failure for example is defined as the first instance at which performance falls below a specified acceptable level.

A particularity in the analysis of survival data relates to the possibility that some individuals may not be observed for the full time to failure. For example, at the close of a life-testing experiment in industrial reliability, not all components may have failed that might eventually fail. Such incomplete observation of the failure time is called censoring (Cox and Oakes 1984). If—as in the example above—on a timeline the individuals' true lifetimes are to the right of the censor time, the observations are right-censored[17] (Smith 2002).

---

[17] For completeness I note that observations may also be left-censored or left/right-truncated. However, for the purpose of this study only right-censoring is of importance.

In general survival analysis is divided into three broad categories:
1) Nonparametric models are rather descriptive in nature and make no assumptions about the hazard function or the influence of covariates. An example is the Kaplan-Meier survival analysis (Kaplan and Meier 1958).
2) Semi-parametric models also do not make assumptions about the hazard function. However, an integral part of semi-parametric models is to make assumption about how covariates affect the hazard function. A primary approach to semi-parametric survival analysis is Cox regression (Cox 1972), which I subsequently introduce and use for the empirical testing.
3) Parametric models require—apart from the assumption that covariates are influencing the hazard function—that the baseline hazard function is specified before estimating the model.

6.2.2 Model specifications

In the following I use a Cox hazard modeling approach to look for more conclusive evidence, which recognizes the different duration it takes a story to reach the popular status (if at all) and that stories may not reach that status within the observation period.

Consistent with the hypotheses H1-H3, my focus is on how the covariates that represent submitters' network characteristics affect the likelihood of a story reaching popular status, as exemplified by the hazard rate. I therefore observe a story up to a fixed cutoff time which I set at 24 hours after the last story in the dataset was submitted. Descriptive statistics show that the time it takes for a story to become popular (reach front page) varies from only fraction of an hour to more than 48 hours. About 95% of the stories reach popular status within 24 hours. Hence, in my data, several stories are right-censored at the time when observation closes.

I propose that the time to popularity for each story and the covariates are related through the following proportional hazard model:

$$h_i(t) = [h_0(t)] \exp(b_0 + b_1 x_{i1} + ... + b_j x_{ij})$$

where $h_i(t)$ is the hazard rate for the ith story at time t, $[h_0(t)]$ is the baseline hazard rate at time t, b_j is the value of the jth regression coefficient and x_{ij} is the value of the ith case of the jth covariate. The hazard function is a measure of story i to get popular at time t given that the story has not become popular.

The baseline hazard rate measures this potential independently of the covariates and thus defines the shape of the hazard function for all cases. The covariates in turn determine the overall magnitude of the function.

While the baseline hazard is dependent on time, the effect of the covariates I subsequently introduce is time independent. Thus, the ratio of the hazards for any two cases at any given point of time is the ratio of the effects of their covariates. This is the proportional hazards assumption which I maintain.

The first hypothesis H1 is based on the size of network (number of members in the network). There is huge variance in network size across users (see Table 4) and the distribution is skewed (see Figure 7, Appendix 2). Thus, I categorize the network size by using the descriptive statistic measures for network size, namely, its mean=81.54 and SD=605.788. This results in the following five categories (frequencies of stories are given in parentheses): category 1 = 0 members (53,757), category 2 = between 1-81members (55,683), category 3 = 82-687 members (5,671), category 4 = 688-1293 members (796) and category 5 = 1294+ members (1717). The other variables used as covariates are self-explanatory from the Tables 4-6 of model results (content categories and media type).

6.2.3 Model results for network size and structure

Model 1a (see Table 5) shows that the network size is highly significant in explaining the chance of a story getting popular (compared to the benchmark 0 network), supporting H1a-b. I check how the results change in the presence of content and message factors in model 1b, to be described later. The impact of the successive higher network size is stronger as well (category 2 over 1: estimated coefficient is 2.24, category 3 over 1 it is 5.98, category 4 over 1 it is 7.69 and category 5 over 1 it is 8.46), as hypothesized.

Model 2a depicts that friends and fans both have a highly significant influence on the likelihood of popularity. Furthermore, to check the relative impact of friends and fans, I also ran model 2a with standardized numbers of friends and fans. The estimates for friends is .377 (.008)***, for fans .279 (.010)*** and for the interaction term -.027 (.003)***. This comparison of the standardized beta estimates indicates the higher influence of friends relative to fans in explaining the likelihood of a story becoming popular. Thus, this is supportive of H2. The results of model 2a in Table 5 are supportive of H3. This is through the highly significant negative estimated coefficient for the interaction term.

Moreover, I present model 3a to show how friends relative to fans influence the likelihood of popularity, in the presence of network size. Note that network size correlates with number of friends and fans, and thus I use the ratio of number of friends to number of fans as the appropriate covariate (which *a priori* does not correlate with network size) in model 3a. Looking at the estimated coefficients I find that network size remains a strong contributor, and that the ratio is, as expected, highly significant and negative in sign.

An overall comparison of the three models suggest that models 3a produce a better but still comparable log-likelihood in relation to model 1a (-2LL of 14531 and 14678, with the 3a estimating an additional parameter), while the model 2a produces considerably worse outcome (-2LL of 17355).

Table 5: Results for models 1a – 3a

Variable	Model 1a	Model 2a	Model 3a
Network dummy 1 (1-81)	2.242 (.525)***		2.444 (.525)***
Network dummy 2 (82-687)	5.984 (.506)***		6.638 (.507)***
Network dummy 3 (688-1,293)	7.687 (.508)***		7.927 (.509)***
Network dummy 4 (1294-max)	8.462 (.502)***		8.508 (.502)***
ratio Friends/Fans			-.566 (.086)***
Friends		7.46E-3(2.00E-4)***	
Fans		4.79E-4(1.41E-5)***	
Friends*Fans		-9.15E-7 (9.90E-8)***	
-2LL	14,678.509	17,355.057	14,531.345
-2LL for null model	19,626.612		

* $p < .05$, ** $p < .01$, *** $p < .001$

Recall that I posit in H1a and H2 that the effects of network characteristics occur irrespective of content and message factors. Thus, I estimate the models 1a-3a by including dummy variables for type of content and type of media (both as designated by Digg). Note that the submitter chooses under which category the content appears. The types of content are: technology, world & business, science, gaming, lifestyle, entertainment, sports and offbeat, as provided by Digg. Media types are: news, image and video.

The results are presented in Table 6. It is striking to note that there is almost no improvement in overall measure of fit from models 1a, 2a and 3a (-2 LL in order are 14678, 17355, 14531) to models 1b, 2b and 3b (-2LL in order are 14524, 17040, 14373) respectively. Moreover, comparison of the estimated coefficients between each pair of models (1a with 1b, 2a with 2b, and 3a with 3b in Table 5 and 6) show very little change in the values.

Table 6: Results for model 1b – 3b

Variable		Model 1b	Model 2b	Model 3b
Network dummy 1 (1-81)		2.277 (.525)***		2.472 (.525)***
Network dummy 2 (82-687)		6.063 (.506)***		6.749 (.508)***
Network dummy 3 (688-1293)		7.729 (.509)***		7.953 (.510)***
Network dummy 4 (1294-max)		8.377 (.502)***		8.423 (.502)***
ratio Friends/Fans				-.530 (.082)***
Friends			7.55E-3 (2.07E-4)***	
Fans			4.29E-4 (1.50E-5)***	
Friends*Fans			-7.41E-7 (1.00E-7)***	
Topic	Gaming	-.051 (.190)	.315 (.190)	-.080 (.191)
(ref. cat. =	Lifestyle	-.012 (.132)	-.141 (.132)	-.046 (.131)
Entertainment)	Offbeat	-.059 (.131)	.367 (.132)**	-.116 (.131)
	Science	.522 (.135)***	1.421 (.135)***	.478 (.134)***
	Sports	.214 (.169)	.369 (.170)*	.152 (.169)
	Technology	.275 (.129)*	.546 (.129)***	.171 (.129)
	World&Business	-.745(.139)***	-.478 (.141)***	-.848 (.139)***
Media	Images	.278 (.134)*	.406 (.138)**	.264 (.134)*
(ref. cat. = Video)	News	-.242 (113)	-.548 (.114)***	-.217 (.113)
-2LL		14,524.984	17,040.769	14,373.467
-2LL null model 19,626.612				

* $p < .05$, ** $p < .01$, *** $p < .001$

This provides first evidence that type of content and media play an unusually secondary role when it comes to propagation of information toward reaching popularity status. Hence, the influence of network characteristics on popularity seems to happen irrespective of content and message factors, as hypothesized in H1-H3. Note that I also tested submission time of day and day of week as covariates. However, I observed only weak and mostly non-significant effects. Moreover, the improvement of -2LL is only 42 if seven dummy variables for three-hour blocks as well as 6 dummy variables for the days of the week are added to model 6.

It is important to recognize that besides the network based effects there could be influence from the past effectiveness of the submitter. Thus, I do a robustness check of the three models by using the covariate "Hit Rate" (defined as number of popular stories submitted by a user divided by total number of stories submitted by the user *in the previous 4 weeks*) which is based on dataset 3.

Table 7 (see also Table 6) shows that there is considerable improvement in overall fit from models 1b and 3b to models 4 and 6 (-2LL 14,524 to 13,763, and 14,373 to 13,666). However, the improvement is big from model 2b to model 5 (-2LL change from 17041 to 14710). Importantly, the significance of network size, and friends and fans remain as before. This provides further evidence of the influence of the egocentric network on whether and how a submitted story becomes popular through the local cascade phase. Additionally the improvement of fit shows that the models using the network dummies are superior to the model using the absolute number of friends and fans.

So far, the tested models take into account aspects of network size and structure. As control variables I added content categories and media type (as provided by Digg), as well as the past hit rate, as described above.

However, two major issues remain with the chosen approach. 1) The model does not take into account the actual activity of the users but just the size and structure of the submitter's network and 2) the content categories are a broad and somewhat unsatisfying measure in terms of controlling for content. I address these issues in the following two chapters.

Table 7: Results for model 4 -6

Variable		Model 4	Model 5	Model 6
Network dummy 1 (1-81)		2.250 (.525)***		2.410 (.525)***
Network dummy 2 (82-687)		5.831 (.507)***		6.335 (.509)***
Network dummy 3 (688-1293)		6.360 (.514)***		6.531 (.514)***
Network dummy 4 (1294-max)		6.819 (.507)***		6.928 (.507)***
ratio Friends/Fans				-.341 (.067)***
Friends			7.00E-3 (2.94E-4)***	
Fans			3.77E-4 (2.43E-5)***	
Friends*Fans			-1.45E-6 (1.55E-7)***	
Topic	Gaming	.206 (.190)	.384 (.190)*	.228 (.190)
(ref. cat. =	Lifestyle	.002 (.131)	-.014 (.132)	-.023 (.131)
Entertainment)	Offbeat	.009 (.131)	.273 (.132)*	-.036 (.132)
	Science	.383 (.134)**	.772 (.135)***	.351 (.134)**
	Sports	.067 (.170)	.268 (.169)	.016 (.170)
	Technology	.236 (.128)	.375 (.128)*	.138 (.128)
	World&Business	-.227(.139)	.034 (.138)	-.326 (.140)*
Media	Images	.019 (.136)	-.159 (.138)	.026 (.136)
(ref. cat. =	News	-.316 (112)	-.597 (.112)***	-.295 (.112)**
Video)				
Past hit rate		4.318 (.150)***	6.721 (.117)***	4.137 (.148)***
-2LL		13,763.441	14,710.695	13,666.304
-2LLnull model	19,626.612			

* $p < .05$, ** $p < .01$, *** $p < .001$

Note—Past hit rate is the ratio of popular stories divided by the total number of submitted stories. This refers to the 4 weeks preceding Sept $14^{th} - 20^{th}$.

6.2.4 Model results for user activity

So far, I have considered different covariates relating to network size and structure as well as different control variables. These are static measures relating to the configuration of the submitter's network at time of submission. However, the descriptive results have shown that friends tend to vote more (number of diggs) and more often (number of voted stories) than fans. To expand the existing hazard model and to better analyze the impact of user actions, I add several measures that take into account not only the total numbers of friends and fans but also their voting behavior. This allows for a different approach to address H 2.

More specifically, I have collected and transformed data that allows me to measure the number of diggs in the upcoming stage of the story lifecycle. For the majority of the stories that never make the transition to the popular stage, the corresponding number is the number of diggs at time of data collection, subdivided into friends and fans. For the popular stories (the stories that get promoted to the front page) it is the number of diggs at popular time, i.e. the second that the story got promoted to the front page. Given those numbers, I can define the following measures (variable name in brackets):

1) Number of diggs by friends in the upcoming stage (diggsFriendsUp) and the number of diggs by fans in the upcoming stage (diggsFansUp).
2) Proportion of friends digging in the upcoming stage to number of upcoming diggs (PropFriendsUpDiggsUp) proportion of fans digging in the upcoming stage to number of upcoming diggs (PropFansUpDiggsUp).

The problem with approach 1) is the high correlation (.806***) of the two variables which would cause mulitcollinearity if they were included as covariates into the hazard model. Hence, I use the aggregated measure of diggs by friends and fans, i.e. the network, in the upcoming stage. Even though this does not allow me to distinguish between the two groups—and thus does not serve to test H2—it provides support to test the general notion that the submitters' networks are of crucial influence as stated in H1. Additionally I run separate models for DiggsFriendsUp and DiggsFansUp to observe how using the two variables as covariates affects model fit. For 2) the problem of multicollinearity does not exist as the correlation between PropFriendsUpDiggsUp and PropFansUpDiggsUp is .187***.

The best measure to test H2 in this model are the ratios in 2) as these ratios indicate which proportion of the votes in the upcoming stage is derived from the group of friends and the group of fans. They are not only for practical reasons better measures than the numbers in 1) but also consider the variance that is caused by the Digg promotion algorithm. As no absolute number of diggs exists that causes success, it is best to included relative measures related to the upcoming diggs that were needed to promote a story to the frontpage.

In the following, I focus on models using network categories instead of the number of friends and fans as covariates. Models 1 – 6 have shown the better fit of the earlier approach. If considering user actions, the simplest and broadest measure is the number of diggs in the upcoming stage—not subdividing this number into diggs by friends, fans or non-network users. Hence, I include this number (DiggsUpcoming) in models 7-9 (Table 24 and 25, Appendix 2). Model 7a just takes into account the network dummies and is extended in model 8a by the ratio friends/fans. In model 9a I add the content categories and media type. For models 7a-9a -2LL is 14,265, 14,160 and 14,076 respectively. The improvement of -2LL over models 1a, 3a and 3b (the comparable models without the additional covariate DiggsUpcoming) is 414, 371 and 297 respectively. The estimated coefficients for Diggs count upcoming are .015(.001)***, .014(.001)*** and .013(.001)*** for 7a-9a. Models 7-9b differ from 7a-9a by the past hit rate. For Models 7b-9b -2LL is 13,784, 13,697 and 13,656. Adding the past hit rate to the model therefore brings an improvement of 481, 464 and 420 (for models 7b-9b over 7a-9a). The estimated coefficients are .004(.001)***, .003(.001)*** and .003(.001)** for 7-9b.

In the following, these numbers serve as a benchmark to see how the different ratios improve the fit of the models and how the coefficients turn out. Next, I use the sum of number of diggs by friends and fans in the upcoming stage, i.e. the diggs by the network (see Table 8 and 9). Adding this number as a covariate, the models do worse than using the DiggsCountUpcoming. -2LL is 177, 162 and 148 higher for models 10a-12a compared to 7a-9a. The improvement of models 10a-12a is therefore only 236, 210 and 150 if compared to models 1a, 3a and 3b. The estimated coefficients for DiggsNetworkUpcoming are .018(.001)***, .017(.001)*** and .015(.001)*** and thus effects seem comparable.

Table 8: Results for models 10a - 12a

Variable		Model 10a	Model 11a	Model 12a
Network dummy 1 (1-81)		2.234 (.525)***	2.415 (.525)***	2.441 (.525)***
Network dummy 2 (82-687)		5.970 (.506)***	6.536 (.508)***	6.617 (.508)***
Network dummy 3 (688-1293)		7.231 (.511)***	7.408 (.511)***	7.435 (.513)***
Network dummy 4 (1294-max)		7.482 (.508)***	7.584 (.508)***	7.595 (.508)***
ratio Friends/Fans			-.443 (.077)***	-.427 (.074)***
DiggsNetworkUpcoming		.018 (.001)***	.017 (.001)***	.015 (.001)***
Topic	Gaming			.020 (.190)
(ref. cat. =	Lifestyle			-.050 (.130)
Entertainment)	Offbeat			-.097 (.131)
	Science			.513 (.134)
	Sports			-.022 (.170)***
	Technology			.172 (.128)
	World&Business			-.603 (.140)***
Media	Images			.227 (.134)
(ref. cat. =	News			-.221 (.112)*
Video)				
-2LL		14,442.341	14,321.675	14,223.283
-2LL null model	19626.612			

* $p < .05$, ** $p < .01$, *** $p < .001$

However, adding the past hit rate in 10b-12b changes the structure (see Table 9). In 10b -2LL is only 3.6 higher compared to 7b. For 11b and 12b the fit is even better than for 8b and 9b with –2LL improvements of 6 and 10. Even if this difference is marginal, it is surprising as the models taking into account the DiggsCountUpcoming and not considering the past hit rate, did considerably better than the models having the DiggsNetworkUpcoming as a covariate. After adding the past hit rate this difference does not exist anymore.

A look at the coefficients reveals that the effect of DiggsNetworkUpcoming turns negative with estimates of -.006(.001)***, -.006(.001)*** and -.007(.002)*** respectively.

Table 9: Results for models 10b – 12b

Variable		Model 10b	Model 11b	Model 12b
Network dummy 1 (1-81)		2.225 (.525)***	2.389 (.525)***	2.413 (.525)***
Network dummy 2 (82-687)		5.894 (.506)***	6.381 (.508)***	6.455 (.509)***
Network dummy 3 (688-1293)		6.673 (.514)***	6.848 (.514)***	6.858 (.516)***
Network dummy 4 (1294-max)		7.088 (.509)***	7.210 (.509)***	7.226 (.510)***
ratio Friends/Fans			-.357 (.069)***	-.356 (.068)***
DiggsNetworkUpcoming		-.006 (.001)***	-.006 (.001)***	-.007 (.002)***
Topic	Gaming			.185 (.190)
(ref. cat. =	Lifestyle			.017 (.130)
Entertainment)	Offbeat			-.043 (.131)
	Science			.319 (.134)
	Sports			.073 (.170)*
	Technology			.168 (.128)
	World&Business			-.400 (.141)
Media	Images			-.003 (.136)**
(ref. cat. =	News			-.284 (.112)*
Video)				
Past hit rate		4.745 (.162)***	4.616 (.160)***	4.476 (.165)***
-2LL		13787.443	13690.547	13644.720
-2LL null model	19626.612			

* $p < .05$, ** $p < .01$, *** $p < .001$

These above stated results indicated that the absolute number of diggs (whether all upcoming diggs or diggs by the network) might not serve as an adequate covariate, as assumed earlier. To test the robustness of this assumption, I additionally tested the models from the previous step for friends and fans individually (see Table 26–29, Appendix 2). In models 13-15 I use diggs by friends as a covariate. Comparing models 13a-15a to 10-12a shows the new models do marginally better with -2LL improvements of 16, 17 and 16 compared to the models taking into account the diggs by network. The coefficients for the new models are .022(.001)***, .020(.001)*** and .018(.001)***. Adding the past hit rate, leads to comparable results as seen in the previous step. –2LL improvements are comparable and the difference is only marginal (9, 10 and 12 of models 13-15b compared to models 10-12b). Again, the coefficients change sign and the estimates are -.004(.002)**, -.005(.002)** and -.005 (.002)**.

Models 16-18 (Table 28 and 29, Appendix 2) differ only by the fact that the number of diggs by fans is used as a covariate instead of the number of diggs by friends. For models 16a-18a the fit is worse than for 13-15a. Comparing 16a-18a to models 10a-12a shows that -2LL is considerably higher (175, 161 and 125). Note that using diggs by friends instead of diggs by fans results in a lower -2LL. The estimates for the coefficients are .037(.005)***, .033(.005)*** and .025(.005)***. Adding the past hit rate again returns coefficients that change signs. The results are -.031(.005)***, -.033(.005)*** and -.036(.006)*** respectively. Again, -2LL is very close to the results of models 10b-12b. For model 16b and 17b the fit is slightly better (by 19 and 20), for 18b -2LL is marginally larger and therefore worse (by 26).

Next, I include the variables explained in 2), i.e. the proportion of friends digging in the upcoming stage to number of upcoming diggs (PropFriendsUpDiggsUp) and the proportion of fans digging in the upcoming stage to number of upcoming diggs (PropFansUpDiggsUp). Comparing models 19a – 21a to models 1a, 3a and 3b (the reference model without PropFriendsUpDiggsUp and PropFansUpDiggsUp) the improvement of -2LL is 251, 243 and 206 respectively. In relation to the improvement that the introduction of DiggsCountUpcoming brings (models 7a – 9a), models 19a-20a don't do quite as good. The difference in -2LL is 162, 128 and 92.

However, comparing them to models 10a-12a (diggs by network) shows a slightly better fit of models 19-21a (15.186, 33.334 and 55.635). The coefficients for PropFriendsUpDiggsUp are 2.861(.187)***, 2.805(.191)*** and 2.670(.197)***. All three estimates for PropFansUpDiggsUp are non-significant.

Table 10: Results for models 19a – 21a

Variable		Model 19a	Model 20a	Model 21a
Network dummy 1 (1-81)		2.113 (.525)***	2.351 (.525)***	2.379 (.525)***
Network dummy 2 (82-687)		5.412 (.510)***	6.081 (.512)***	6.142 (.513)***
Network dummy 3 (688-1293)		6.594 (.518)***	6.845 (.519)***	6.855 (.521)***
Network dummy 4 (1294-max)		7.178 (.515)***	7.311 (.516)***	7.263 (.517)***
ratio Friends/Fans			-.562 (.089)***	-.502 (.084)***
PropFriendsUpDiggsUp		2.861 (.187)***	2.805 (.191)***	2.670 (.197)***
PropFansUpDiggsUp		.466 (.407)	-.038 (.419)	-.034 (.437)
Topic	Gaming			-.086 (.192)
(ref. cat. =	Lifestyle			-.059 (.130)
Entertainment)	Offbeat			-.106 (.131)
	Science			.535 (.134)***
	Sports			.065 (.170)
	Technology			.231 (.129)
	World&Business			-.621 (.140)***
Media	Images			.285 (.134)*
(ref. cat. =	News			-.252 (.113)*
Video)				
-2LL		14,427.155	14,288.341	14,167.648
-2LL null model	19,626.612			

* $p < .05$, ** $p < .01$, *** $p < .001$

This strongly supports H2, where I posit that the submitter's friends are more influential than the submitter's fans. Adding the past hit rate, the estimates for PropFriendsUpDiggsUp stay highly significant and positive (1.353(.225)***, 1.217(.227)*** and 1.193(.230)***) while the estimates for PropFansUpDiggsUp become significant and negative (-1.058(.473)*, -1.529(.488)**, -1.609(.490)**). Note that for all the other models tested in this essay that consider friend and fan activity as covariates, the sign of the coefficients changes when past hit rate is introduced. This further supports the assumption of the strong influence of friends.

Table 11: Results for model 19b – 21b

Variable		Model 19b	Model 20b	Model 21b
Network dummy 1 (1-81)		2.198 (.525)***	2.376 (.525)***	2.393 (.525)***
Network dummy 2 (82-687)		5.643 (.509)***	6.177 (.512)***	6.205 (.513)***
Network dummy 3 (688-1293)		6.073 (.523)***	6.333 (.524)***	6.302 (.525)***
Network dummy 4 (1294-max)		6.496 (.519)***	6.715 (.519)***	6.704 (.520)***
ratio Friends/Fans			-.367 (.072)***	-.356 (.070)***
PropFriendsUpDiggsUp		1.353 (.225)***	1.217 (.227)***	1.193 (.230)***
PropFansUpDiggsUp		-1.058 (.473)*	-1.529 (.488)**	-1.609 (.490)**
Topic	Gaming			.234 (.191)
(ref. cat. =	Lifestyle			.009 (.130)
Entertainment)	Offbeat			-.050 (.132)
	Science			.391 (.134)**
	Sports			.025 (.170)
	Technology			.182 (.128)
	World&Business			-.250 (.141)
Media	Images			.019 (.135)
(ref. cat. =	News			-.330 (.112)**
Video)				
Past hit rate		4.153 (.157)***	4.009 (.156)***	3.872 (.161)***
-2LL		13,754.690	13,661.028	13,618.283
-2LL null model	19,626.612			

* $p < .05$, ** $p < .01$, *** $p < .001$

6.2.5 Model results for content analysis

One of the major assumptions in this essay is that information propagation in the local stage depends on network characteristics, irrespective of content factors. To test this, I included the content categories and the media type provided by Digg as covariates into the hazard model, as discussed earlier. However, trying to control the content with just those categories is an unsatisfying approach, not capturing the variance between submitted stories. Therefore, observing no major increases in model fit if the categories are added as covariates to the model, as well as having only a few significant categories, does not seem the best approach to support H1a and H2.

To better capture aspects of content, I therefore apply automated content analysis, as detailed in the following.

The Linguistic Inquiry and Word Count (LIWC) developed by Pennebaker, Francis and Booth (2007) is a text analysis software used extensively for research in nonclinical populations (see Lee et al. 2007, Fivush et al. 2007, Humphreys 2010, Brett et al. 2007, Berger and Milkman 2010). The program calculates the percentage of words within several categories that are used within the provided text. The underlying logic is that the program searches for groups of words that have been predefined as matching the various categories. "For example, the program searches for and counts words that are related to the construct of anger. Groups of judges were used who agreed that words such as *hate, kill, angry, outrage*, and so on were all anger-related words" (Pennebaker and Chung 2009, p. 454). All the categories provided by LIWC are displayed in Table 30 (Appendix 2).

To be able to implement this type of automated content analysis, I content-analyzed title and description of the stories individually and then calculated the weighted average of both. I applied this approach for two reasons:

1) It seems reasonable to argue that the content of a story is assessed both by its title and description. As the title is typically much shorter than the description I applied the weighted average.
2) Some content, especially videos and pictures, doesn't have a description.

Thus, for purposes of data preparation, a total of 68 variables were calculated for each story. Apart from the first five categories of linguistic processes (where the total number was counted), percentages were calculated for all variables. Or in other words, how many percent of words of the combined description and title were found in the respective categories.

Not surprisingly, some of the 68 variables show very high correlations, which make the direct use as covariates impossible. Therefore I apply the following approaches to be able to use the results of the content analysis as control variables:
1) Use of just the main categories. The 68 categories provided by LIWC show a hierarchy (as indicated in Table 30), where some categories are subcategories of others (e.g. 1st person singular is a subcategory of personal pronouns is a subcategory of total pronouns is a subcategory of total function words). In this approach I use "word count, total function words, swear words, social processes, affective processes, cognitive processes, perceptual processes, biological processes, relativity, work, achievement, leisure, home, money, religion, death, assent, nonfluencies, fillers". All of the correlations are smaller than .5.
2) Principal Components Analysis. I apply a factor analysis to reduce dimensions and circumvent the problem of multicollinearity.

The results of approach 1) are displayed in Table 12. Comparing models 25a-27a to 1a, 3a and 3b (the reference models) shows that adding the text categories brings only a small improvement of model fit. -2LL changes by only 44, 43 and 49. Out of the 19 variables, only four have a significant estimate (in model 25a). Adding the other parameters to the model results in three significant coefficients, while in model 27a four of the content categories turn out to have a significant influence. The other coefficients are comparable to model 3b. Adding the past hit rate brings larger model improvements. -2LL of 25b-27b improves by 860, 806 and 694 compared to 25a-27a. As a comparison, adding the past hit rate to models 7a-9a (DiggsUpcoming) improves -2LL by 420-481; adding it to 19a-21a (PropFriends/FansDiggUp) improves -2LL by 510-564. This indicates that the explanatory power of the main categories is smaller than of the other referenced measures.

In approach 2) I use principal components extracted from the 68 variables as covariates. Factors with Eigenvalues greater than 1 were extracted (See Table 31, Appendix 2, for Eigenvalues and Figure 8, Appendix 2, for the scree plot). The rotated component matrix (Varimax rotation) is shown in Table 32, Appendix 2.

Table 12: Results for models 25a – 27a

Variable		Model 25a	Model 26a	Model 27a
Network dummy 1 (1-81)		2.187 (.525)***	2.390 (.525)***	2.417 (.525)***
Network dummy 2 (82-687)		5.969 (.506)***	6.602 (.508)***	6.687 (.508)***
Network dummy 3 (688-1293)		7.736 (.509)***	7.925 (.509)***	7.926 (.510)***
Network dummy 4 (1294-max)		8.372 (.503)***	8.414 (.503)***	8.294 (.503)***
ratio Friends/Fans			-.533 (.084)***	-.501 (.080)***
Topic (ref. cat. = Entertainment)	Gaming			-.099 (.192)
	Lifestyle			-.109 (.136)
	Offbeat			-.163 (.135)
	Science			.457 (.142)**
	Sports			.119 (.173)
	Technology			.144 (.135)
	World&Business			-.930 (.147)***
Media (ref. cat. = Video)	Images			.288 (.136)*
	News			-.313 (.116)**
Content categories	WC	-.001 (.001)	-.001 (.001)	.000 (.001)
	funct	.010 (.003)**	.010 (.004)**	.012 (.004)***
	swear	-.010 (.049)	-.010 (.049)	-.009 (.049)
	social	-.014 (.007)*	-.013 (.007)	-.005 (.007)
	affect	.017 (.008)*	.017 (.008)*	.019 (.008)*
	cogmech	-.004 (.006)	-.003 (.006)	-.003 (.006)
	percept	.001 (.012)	.001 (.012)	-.012 (.012)
	bio	.007 (.010)	.010 (.010)	.013 (.010)
	achieve	-.016 (.013)	-.015 (.013)	-.017 (.013)
	leisure	.010 (.009)	.013 (.009)	.001 (.010)
	home	-.038 (.026)	-.040 (.026)	-.029 (.025)
	relig	-.031 (.030)	-.025 (.030)	.007 (.030)
	death	-.060 (.031)	-.057 (.031)	-.016 (.030)
	relativ	.016 (.005)**	.016 (.005)**	.020 (.005)***
	work	-.001 (.010)	-.001 (.010)	.015 (.009)
	money	-.013 (.013)	-.012 (.013)	.021 (.013)
	assent	-.019 (.043)	-.020 (.043)	-.043 (.043)
	nonfl	-.065 (.081)	-.070 (.082)	-.093 (.081)
	filler	.018 (.047)	.015 (.047)	.003 (.046)
-2LL		14,634.028	14,488.131	14,324.578
-2LL null model 19,626.612				

* $p < .05$, ** $p < .01$, *** $p < .001$

Table 13: Results for models 25b – 27b

Variable		Model 25b		Model 26b		Model 27b	
Network dummy 1 (1-81)		2.189	(.525)***	2.352	(.525)***	2.369	(.525)***
Network dummy 2 (82-687)		5.803	(.507)***	6.273	(.508)***	6.312	(.509)***
Network dummy 3 (688-1293)		6.415	(.514)***	6.571	(.514)***	6.509	(.515)***
Network dummy 4 (1294-max)		6.796	(.508)***	6.901	(.508)***	6.861	(.508)***
ratio Friends/Fans				-.345	(.069)***	-.342	(.068)***
Topic (ref. cat. = Entertainment)	Gaming					.246	(.192)
	Lifestyle					-.030	(.136)
	Offbeat					-.089	(.136)
	Science					.296	(.143)*
	Sports					-.009	(.173)
	Technology					.183	(.134)
	World&Business					-.428	(.149)**
Media (ref. cat. = Video)	Images					.034	(.138)
	News					-.363	(.115)**
Content categories	WC	.000	(.001)	.000	(.001)	.000	(.001)
	funct	.007	(.003)	.006	(.003)	.009	(.004)*
	swear	-.014	(.053)	-.014	(.052)	-.010	(.052)
	social	-.008	(.007)	-.007	(.007)	-.002	(.007)
	affect	.013	(.008)	.013	(.008)	.015	(.008)
	cogmech	-.013	(.006)*	-.011	(.006)	-.012	(.006)
	percept	-.006	(.012)	-.006	(.012)	-.014	(.013)
	bio	.006	(.010)	.007	(.010)	.011	(.010)
	achieve	-.016	(.013)	-.016	(.013)	-.018	(.013)
	leisure	-.007	(.009)	-.005	(.009)	-.013	(.010)
	home	-.055	(.025)*	-.056	(.025)*	-.051	(.025)*
	relig	.003	(.029)	.006	(.030)	.022	(.029)
	death	-.033	(.030)	-.035	(.030)	-.017	(.029)
	relativ	.013	(.005)**	.014	(.005)**	.016	(.005)**
	work	.006	(.010)	.006	(.010)	.014	(.010)
	money	-.011	(.012)	-.011	(.012)	.004	(.012)
	assent	-.033	(.042)	-.034	(.042)	-.046	(.042)
	nonfl	-.057	(.082)	-.058	(.082)	-.091	(.084)
	filler	.000	(.049)	-.002	(.049)	-.007	(.049)
	Past hitrate	4.415	(.1649)***	4.249	(.145)***	4.073	(.150)***
-2LL		13774.054		13681.935		13630.132	
-2LL null model	19626.612						

* $p < .05$, ** $p < .01$, *** $p < .001$

In approach 2) I use principal components extracted from the 68 variables as covariates. Factors with Eigenvalues greater than 1 were extracted (See Table 31, Appendix 2, for Eigenvalues and Figure 8, Appendix 2, for the scree plot). The rotated component matrix (Varimax rotation) is shown in Table 32, Appendix 2.

The use of the 24 factors as covariates in models 28a-30a returns very comparable results to approach 1). Improvements of -2LL in relation to the reference models 1a, 3a and 3b are 50, 48 and 72, with five to six of the factors shown significant effects. I detail these factors in the following. Factor 1 has a positive coefficient and consists of: verbs, auxiliary verbs, present tense, total function words and impersonal pronouns.

Factor 2 has the largest positive coefficient, is highly significant and consists of: relativity, space, preposition and dictionary words. Factor 4 has a negative coefficient and consists of: personal pronouns, total pronouns, second person and arguably first person singular. Factor 9 has a positive coefficient and consists of: exclusive, negations and tentative. Factor 13 only has a significant influence if the content categories are not included and consists of: sadness and arguably achievement. Factor 18 is only significant when content categories are added to the model and consists of: past tense and third person singular. Adding the hit rate in model 28b-30b again brings very comparable results to the models 25b-27b (see Table 15). In terms of -2LL models 28b-30b do better by 12-24, an only marginal improvement. Fewer factors are significant in the b-models but those that are, have also been significant before the past hit rate was introduced in the a-models. Coefficients are comparable and no change of sings can be observed.

Table 14: Results for models 28a – 30a

Variable		Model 28a	Model 29a	Model 30a
Network dummy 1 (1-81)		2.173 (.525)***	2.379 (.525)***	2.393 (.525)***
Network dummy 2 (82-687)		5.936 (.506)***	6.572 (.508)***	6.624 (.508)***
Network dummy 3 (688-1293)		7.698 (.509)***	7.891 (.510)***	7.849 (.510)***
Network dummy 4 (1294-max)		8.318 (.503)***	8.365 (.503)***	8.205 (.503)***
ratio Friends/Fans			-.533 (.084)***	-.494 (.080)***
Topic (ref. cat. = Entertainment)	Gaming			-.080 (.193)
	Lifestyle			-.045 (.136)
	Offbeat			-.188 (.135)
	Science			.493 (.142)*
	Sports			.110 (.173)
	Technology			.265 (.136)
	World&Business			-.927 (.146)**
Media (ref. cat. = Video)	Images			.342 (.136)*
	News			-.335 (.116)**
Content components	FAC1	.086 (.040)*	.090 (.040)*	.135 (.040)**
	FAC2	.183 (.041)***	.185 (.041)***	.252 (.042)***
	FAC3	.025 (.056)	.020 (.056)	-.009 (.055)
	FAC4	-.088 (.038)*	-.076 (.038)*	-.088 (.038)*
	FAC5	.006 (.041)	.015 (.040)	.037 (.041)
	FAC6	.008 (.039)	.009 (.039)	.034 (.039)
	FAC7	.007 (.041)	.006 (.042)	-.068 (.042)
	FAC8	.024 (.041)	.030 (.041)	.029 (.040)
	FAC9	.082 (.030)**	.077 (.030)*	.095 (.029)**
	FAC10	-.050 (.039)	-.037 (.040)	-.039 (.040)
	FAC11	.007 (.029)	.003 (.029)	.062 (.029)*
	FAC12	.023 (.042)	.034 (.043)	.048 (.043)
	FAC13	.064 (.032)*	.067 (.033)*	.041 (.031)
	FAC14	.013 (.031)	.015 (.031)	.025 (.031)
	FAC15	.029 (.035)	.031 (.035)	.060 (.035)
	FAC16	.021 (.034)	.019 (.034)	.026 (.034)
	FAC17	-.077 (.045)	-.083 (.045)	.082 (.047)
	FAC18	.035 (.029)	.030 (.029)	.071 (.030)*
	FAC19	.030 (.027)	.033 (.026)	.017 (.027)
	FAC20	-.004 (.036)	-.011 (.036)	.030 (.036)
	FAC21	.043 (.029)	.041 (.028)	.037 (.028)
	FAC22	.002 (.037)	.000 (.037)	-.029 (.037)
	FAC23	.037 (.039)	.039 (.038)	.062 (.038)
	FAC24	-.028 (.036)	-.029 (.036)	.000 (.035)
-2LL		14628.282	14483.236	14301.683
-2LL null model 19626.612				

* $p < .05$, ** $p < .01$, *** $p < .001$

Table 15: Results for models 28b – 30b

Variable		Model 28b	Model 29b	Model 30b
Network dummy 1 (1-81)		2.169 (.525)***	2.334 (.526)***	2.346 (.526)***
Network dummy 2 (82-687)		5.748 (.507)***	6.218 (.509)***	6.238 (.509)***
Network dummy 3 (688-1293)		6.351 (.514)***	6.515 (.514)***	6.435 (.515)***
Network dummy 4 (1294-max)		6.723 (.508)***	6.832 (.508)***	6.773 (.508)***
ratio Friends/Fans			-.343 (.069)***	-.335 (.067)***
Topic (ref. cat. = Entertainment)	Gaming			.279 (.193)
	Lifestyle			.035 (.137)
	Offbeat			-.130 (.137)
	Science			.359 (.143)*
	Sports			-.014 (.174)
	Technology			.329 (.136)*
	World&Business			-.413 (.147)**
Media (ref. cat.= Video)	Images			.110 (.139)
	News			-.363 (.115)**
Content components	FAC1	.061 (.041)	.060 (.041)	.102 (.042)*
	FAC2	.144 (.042)**	.146 (.042)***	.196 (.043)***
	FAC3	-.049 (.059)	-.051 (.059)	-.068 (.057)
	FAC4	-.103 (.040)**	-.095 (.040)*	-.097 (.040)*
	FAC5	.011 (.040)	.014 (.040)	.035 (.042)
	FAC6	-.057 (.040)	-.052 (.040)	-.048 (.041)
	FAC7	-.033 (.042)	-.032 (.043)	-.076 (.043)
	FAC8	-.023 (.041)	-.019 (.041)	-.017 (.041)
	FAC9	.042 (.031)	.040 (.031)	.059 (.031)
	FAC10	-.062 (.040)	-.051 (.040)	-.051 (.041)
	FAC11	.051 (.029)	.044 (.029)	.074 (.029)*
	FAC12	.050 (.041)	.054 (.042)	.057 (.043)
	FAC13	.050 (.036)	.053 (.036)	.041 (.036)
	FAC14	-.031 (.034)	-.028 (.034)	-.016 (.034)
	FAC15	.034 (.035)	.036 (.035)	.068 (.036)
	FAC16	-.002 (.035)	-.006 (.035)	.003 (.035)
	FAC17	-.034 (.044)	-.038 (.044)	.035 (.046)
	FAC18	.050 (.029)	.039 (.029)	.079 (.030)**
	FAC19	.006 (.029)	.007 (.028)	.010 (.029)
	FAC20	.022 (.037)	.015 (.037)	.044 (.037)
	FAC21	.017 (.030)	.016 (.030)	.015 (.029)
	FAC22	-.009 (.037)	-.010 (.037)	-.030 (.037)
	FAC23	.014 (.037)	.017 (.037)	.028 (.036)
	FAC24	.013 (.036)	.011 (.036)	.021 (.036)
Past hit rate		4.434 (.146)***	4.266 (.145)***	4.070 (.150)***
-2LL		13761.063	13670.992	13606.330
-2LL null model	19626.612			

* $p < .05$, ** $p < .01$, *** $p < .001$

Overall, the factor analysis provides unsatisfying results. For example, why does factor 2 (relativity, space, preposition and dictionary words) show the highest influence, while other aspects, like work, leisure, positive or negative emotions, etc. do not have an effect at all? I see this as a general support of my basic assumptions. More conclusive though, model improvements are marginal. However, I conduct another attempt to implement the text analysis that serves a robustness check. For all the 24 components extracted from the 68 variables, I calculate cronbachs alpha to check the reliability of the items measuring the constructs (components) and see if the removal of certain items optimizes the score. In detail, this implies the following steps:

1) Measure alpha for all constructs. Included items with factor loadings higher than .5 are marked yellow, with factor loadings slightly smaller than .5 that I add to the constructs, are marked orange (see Table 32, Appendix 2). The different alphas are displayed in the column *alpha old*.
2) For alphas <.7, remove these items that optimize the scale in a way that the subsequently calculated alphas >.7. Whenever this approach shows success, I note in column *alpha old* which item I remove and note the resulting alpha in the column *alpha new*. Subsequently, I use only these constructs that show alphas >.7
3) Use the mean of the included items to calculate a new variable.

The above steps result in the following new constructs that are generated out of the listed items:

1) verbs, auxiliary verbs, present tense, total function words, impersonal pronouns
2) relativity, space, preposition
3) word count, words per sentence, numbers
4) pronouns, total pronouns, second person, first person singular
5) biological processes, health, ingestion, body
6) inclusive, conjunctions, cognitive processes
7) perceptual processes, see
8) positive emotions, affective processes
9) anger, negative emotions

Descriptive statistics for the 9 new constructs are shown in Table 16 (note that construct 3 consists of variables that are defined by real numbers, not percentages). The use of the constructs 1-9 as covariates returns comparable results as the earlier two approaches.

Table 16: Descriptive statistics for Constructs 1 - 9

	Minimum	Maximum	Mean	SD
CONST1	0	45.00	11.44	7.30
CONST2	0	66.67	8.14	5.33
CONST3	0.67	1035.66	32.88	62.25
CONST4	0	37.50	2.31	2.82
CONST5	0	66.67	0.86	2.01
CONST6	0	42.86	5.13	4.07
CONST7	0	56.25	1.31	2.54
CONST8	0	100.00	3.68	4.30
CONST9	0	50.00	0.89	2.08

The improvement in fit of models 31a-33a over 1a, 3a and 3b is 32, 31 and 48 respectively. Constructs 1, 2 are significant and have positive coefficients of comparable size and construct 4 is significant and negative in sign for all models. Construct 9 is significant only for the model that includes the content categories.

For models 31b-33b, taking into account the past hit rate, constructs 1 and 2 remain to have an influence (apart from construct 1 in model 32b), construct 4 has no significant effect and construct 9 becomes significant for all models. The improvement in model fit is 870, 816 and 696 respectively.

Comparing the three different attempts to integrate the results of the content analysis returns almost identical results. Controlling for past hit rate, the highest difference in -2LL for the three approaches and three different model types is only 24. This is due to the fact that the integration of the results of content analysis doesn't bring a big overall improvement at all. The best results are estimated for model 30a and b.

For 30a, the improvement in -2LL is 72, for 30b it is 49 in relation to 1a and 3b. If one is observing the improvement that 1a (network categories) and 3b (network categories, ratio friends/fans, content categories) show over the null model, the respective numbers are 5,253 and 5,971. Overall, this provides further support for the assumption that information propagation occurs irrespective of content and message factors.

Table 17: Results for models 31a – 33a

Variable		Model 31a	Model 32a	Model 33a
Network dummy 1 (1-81)		2.181 (.525)***	2.386 (.525)***	2.406 (.525)***
Network dummy 2 (82-687)		5.948 (.506)***	6.581 v.508)***	6.665 (.508)***
Network dummy 3 (688-1293)		7.701 (.509)***	7.894 (.509)***	7.894 (.510)***
Network dummy 4 (1294-max)		8.347 (.503)***	8.392 (.503)***	8.259 (.503)***
ratio Friends/Fans			-.538 (.084)***	-.497 (.080)***
Topic (ref. cat. = Entertainment)	Gaming			-.122 (.192)
	Lifestyle			-.097 (.134)
	Offbeat			-.167 (.132)
	Science			.401 (.136)**
	Sports			.100 (.170)
	Technology			.168 (.130)
	World&Business			-.925 (.140)***
Media (ref. cat. = Video)	Images			.295 (.134)*
	News			-.295 (.115)*
Content components	CONST1	.020 (.008)**	.019 (.008)*	.025 (.008)**
	CONST2	.025 (.008)**	.025 (.008)**	.031 (.008)***
	CONST3	-.001 (.001)	-.001 (.001)	.000 (.001)
	CONST4	-.037 (.017)*	-.033 (.016)*	-.043 (.017)**
	CONST5	.014 (.020)	.019 (.020)	.021 (.020)
	CONST6	-.004 (.011)	-.003 (.011)	.001 (.011)
	CONST7	.000 (.016)	.000 (.016)	-.020 (.016)
	CONST8	.006 (.010)	.007 (.010)	.002 (.010)
	CONST9	.021 (.015)	.018 (.014)	.038 (.013)**
-2LL		14646.032	14500.659	14325.844
-2LL null model 19626.612				

* $p < .05$, ** $p < .01$, *** $p < .001$

Table 18: Results for models 31b – 33b

Variable		Model 31b	Model 32b	Model 33b
Network dummy 1 (1-81)		2.181 (.525)***	2.345 (.525)***	2.361 (.525)***
Network dummy 2 (82-687)		5.783 (.507)***	6.251 (.508)***	6.288 (.509)***
Network dummy 3 (688-1293)		6.383 (.514)***	6.542 (.514)***	6.487 (.515)***
Network dummy 4 (1294-max)		6.763 (.508)***	6.866 (.508)***	6.829 (.508)***
ratio Friends/Fans			-.345 (.069)***	-.339 (.067)***
Topic (ref. cat. = Entertainment)	Gaming			.243 (.191)
	Lifestyle			-.011 (.134)
	Offbeat			-.092 (.133)
	Science			.291 (.137)*
	Sports			-.016 (.171)
	Technology			.230 (.130)
	World&Business			-.398 (.141)**
Media (ref. cat. = Video)	Images			.046 (.136)
	News			-.354 (.114)**
Content components	CONST1	.015 (.008)*	.015 (.008)	.020 (.008)**
	CONST2	.023 (.008)**	.023 (.008)**	.028 (.008)***
	CONST3	.000 (.001)	.000 (.001)	.000 (.001)
	CONST4	-.028 (.016)	-.027 (.016)	-.027 (.016)
	CONST5	.011 (.019)	.013 (.019)	.020 (.020)
	CONST6	-.019 (.011)	-.017 (.011)	-.017 (.011)
	CONST7	-.009 (.016)	-.010 (.016)	-.023 (.016)
	CONST8	-.003 (.010)	-.002 (.010)	-.004 (.010)
	CONST9	.038 (.015)*	.034 (.015)*	.043 (.014)**
	Past hitrate	4.416 (.145)***	4.252 (.144)***	4.062 (.150)***
-2LL		13775.990	13684.507	13629.881
-2LL null model	19626.612			

* $p < .05$, ** $p < .01$, *** $p < .001$

6.3 Results for global cascades

Out of the 117,624 stories that form the basis of my analysis for the local cascade, only 846 stories obtained the critical mass of votes and reached the popular status (or the front page). I observed the progress of these 846 stories in the global cascade phase that is, over the next twelve days (until October 2nd, 2009) and collected several available measures. The broadest measure of success of a story can be defined as the total number of users viewing it and thus constitutes the basic dependent variable for testing H4. "Views" refer to the total number of clicks on the story that is referenced and indicates the degree of attention the respective content achieves (or how many people view it).[18] It is important to note that every user viewing the story is counted, whether he is a registered member of Digg or not. I additionally use two other narrower measures which serve as supplemental dependent variables: namely, total number of users voting (diggs) on the story and the total number of users commentating on the story.

To test the influence of submitter's network based activities in the local cascade stage on the overall success of the story in the global cascade phase, I run regression analysis with the independent variable of interest: Ratio of network diggs—that is number of network users out of all users who voted on the story in the local cascade phase[19]. Table 19 shows the regression model results. Three models are presented: model 34 uses the broadest measure of success, namely, total number of views, as the dependent variable, while models 35 and 36 use the narrower measures total number of diggs and total number of comments as the dependent variables.

For completeness, I also use the covariates that represent content and media types. As hypothesized in H4, the significant negative estimated coefficients for the covariate 'Ratio of network diggs' show that the influence of network activities is indeed <u>inverted</u>. This effect occurs consistently across all three dependent variables: number of views, number of diggs and number of comments. For views, diggs and comments I observe a decrease in adjusted R square (.328, .277 and .250) for the three respective models. Also, I find that the content and the media factors have hardly any significance. That is, the higher the proportions of

---

18 While analyzing the number of views I identified a remarkable aspect. One should assume that before voting on a story a user assesses, i.e. reads, it. However, for 12,596 upcoming (but no popular) stories I observe a negative difference of views-diggs, implying that at least one user voted on the story but didn't read it (maximum of -237 views, Mean (SD) of -4.83 (9,67)). I regard this as supportive of my general assumption that information promotion does not build upon the quality centered assessment of content

19 Mean=11.84 hours, SD=8.95 hours, Min=0.34 hours, Max=47.18 hours

votes by users belonging to the submitter's network in the local cascade, the lower the global success of the story.

Additionally, Table 33 (Appendix 2) shows the same models as above with one variable exchanged. Instead of using the ratio of network diggs at time of promotion, I use the ratio of network diggs two hours after submission[20], conditional on the story being upcoming at this point of time. Descriptive statistics have shown that only 30 (or 3.6%) of all the stories in the observation period made the front page in less than two hours. For those stories I used the ratio at the respective time of promotion. The results show that for all three models (40-42) the adjusted R square is very close to that of the three models (34-36) using the ratio at time of promotion. Model 40 is only 0.005 lower in R square than model 34, for models 41 and 42 the difference is 0.007 and 0.003 respectively. Also, the effect of the ratio of network diggs remains highly significant and the value of the coefficients decreases only slightly. Therefore the negative effect of the ratio of network diggs at time of story promotion (on average after 11.84 hours) provides only a marginal increase in both model fit and magnitude of the coefficients over the ratio measured after two hours.

This leads to the conclusion that the ratio of network diggs after two hours already seems to act as a good predictor of the overall success of a story measured after 12 days. However, I note that this finding is somewhat preliminary in nature and should be regarded as an indicator only.

In models 37-39 I additionally introduce the 24 factors that I used in the hazard model. Adjusted R square improves by .057, .039 and .006 for vies, diggs and comments and up to 7 factors turn out to have a significant influence, while the ratio of diggs remains a strong contributor. Even though results are not comparable to the hazard models, there is an indication that content aspects might play a bigger role in the global stage.

The above described results are consistent with my thesis on egocentric networks' influence in propagation of information. Since global success is conditional on reaching popularity status (front page), and reaching front page is being aided by network of the submitter there is a concern that stories, which otherwise might find traction with the universe of all users are not reaching the front page and thus being denied visibility. This could also point to inefficiency in information propagation as being observed on user controlled social news

---

[20] The 2 hour cutoff is chosen arbitrarily. Tests with other cutoff times have shown that the fit in terms of R square does not get a lot better—as it is already very close to the model using the ratio at time of promotion. However, compared to the one hour cutoff, the two hour cutoff brings a significant improvement

sites and suggests a potential hindrance for UGC to have impact on a broader social scale. For a robustness check of the hypotheses I include the network dummies as well as the ratio friends/fans in models 37-39. For 37 and 38 none of these variables turns out significant (Adjusted R square improved by .001 for model 37 and .007 for model 38). For model 39 all the network dummies have significant but negative estimates (Adjusted R square improved by .008 for 9c). This further underlines the basic assumption that information propagation in the local and global stage differs greatly. More specifically, this strongly supports the idea that while in the local stage networks are of crucial importance, they do not play a role in the global stage—or even have a negative influence on success.

Table 19: Results of models 34 - 36

Variable	Model 34 Views	Model 35 Diggs	Model 36 Comments
Intercept	26056.910 (2340.578)***	1786.953 (119.910)***	296.059 (22.243)***
Ratio of net. diggs	-27808.219 (2714.995)***	-1624 (139.091)***	-301.274 (25.801)***
Topic			
Gaming	-343.509 (2733.488)	-100.781 (140.039)	-7.383 (25.977)
Lifestyle	-223.884 (1895.343)	-63.081 (97.100)	-2.105 (18.012)
Offbeat	6241.361 (1903.056)**	149.473 (97.495)	10.469 (18.085)
Science	-3805.758 (1943.068)*	-206.958 (99.545)*	-40.112 (18.465)*
Sports	-3400.298 (2450.174)	-297.931 (125.524)*	-33.095 (23.285)
Technology	-2737.880 (1854.797)	-178.499 (95.023)	-26.453 (17.627)
World & B.	-1610.426 (1999.509)	54.044 (102.436)	117.056 (19.002)***
Media			
Images	-5717.391 (1651.645)**	-353.944 (84.615)***	-34.786 (15.696)*
News	13054.936 (1971.955)***	343.866 (101.025)**	-17.951 (18.740)
Adjusted R2	.328	.277	.250

$p < .05$, ** $p < .01$, *** $p < .001$

Note—The reference category for Topic is entertainment, for Media it is video

Table 20: Results for models 37 - 39

Variable	Model 37 Views	Model 38 Diggs	Model 39 Comments
Intercept	24148.68 (2418.773)***	1712.766 (125.878)***	271.032 (23.910)***
Rat. of net. d.	-25819.4 (2598.387)***	-1528.240 (135.225)***	-283.944 (25.685)***
Topic			
Gaming	562.237 (2660.758)	-54.943 (138.471)	7.902 (26.302)
Lifestyle	1007.867 (1927.488)	26.006 (100.310)	14.414 (19.053)
Offbeat	5378.736 (1947.815)**	154.947 (101.368)	13.896 (19.254)
Science	-1582.22 (2015.694)	-82.549 (104.901)	-20.299 (19.925)
Sports	-2988.29 (2430.022)	-268.810 (126.463)*	-17.647 (24.021)
Technology	-2647.85 (1864.892)	-157.386 (97.053)	-13.360 (18.435)
World&Bus.	-723.087 (2019.326)	90.667 (105.090)	123.852 (19.961)***
Media			
Images	12907.94 (1965.044)**	347.734 (102.265)	-10.198 (19.425)
News	-4276.7 (1690.721)*	-268.629 (87.989)**	-29.642 (16.713)
FAC1	1129.298 (599.240)**	-12.032 (31.186)	4.753 (5.924)
FAC2	-2026.612 (631.870)	-129.524 (32.884)***	-15.276 (6.246)*
FAC3	-1472.031 (891.334)	-125.303 (46.387)**	-6.936 (8.811)
FAC4	926.534 (543.364)	51.341 (28.278)	-9.256 (5.371)
FAC5	-254.269 (574.471)	-21.087 (29.897)	-1.393 (5.679)
FAC6	-1611.854 (550.084)	-92.979 (28.628)**	-12.319 (5.438)*
FAC7	-462.432 (567.512)	-43.402 (29.534)	-6.043 (5.610)
FAC8	1141.566 (574.939)*	15.129 (29.921)	-2.463 (5.683)
FAC9	-289.084 (430.289)	-37.379 (22.393)	-3.727 (4.253)
FAC10	428.589 (590.361)	5.116 (30.724)	-2.211 (5.836)
FAC11	-146.078 (462.203)	.379 (24.054)	11.871 (4.569)**
FAC12	-525.437 (608.489)	7.696 (31.667)	12.262 (6.015)*
FAC13	390.509 (383.645)	-11.454 (19.966)	-1.656 (3.792)
FAC14	-439.437 (432.290)	-22.753 (22.497)	-.793 (4.273)
FAC15	-1427.378 (467.116)**	-76.686 (24.310)**	2.271 (4.617)
FAC16	-849.522 (488.048)	-59.842 (25.399)*	-7.652 (4.824)
FAC17	-458.244 (678.205)	-17.205 (35.295)	-8.956 (6.704)
FAC18	822.499 (433.066)	29.230 (22.538)	3.803 (4.281)
FAC19	382.874 (457.213)	1.659 (23.794)	.174 (4.520)
FAC20	2342.380 (521.151)***	95.335 (27.122)***	-1.550 (5.152)
FAC21	113.386 (366.292)	-13.089 (19.063)	-1.835 (3.621)
FAC22	2321.652 (561.480)***	67.652 (29.221)*	3.807 (5.550)
FAC23	370.228 (541.221)	4.688 (28.166)	-2.712 (5.350)
FAC24	-374.325 (519.292)	-23.157 (27.025)	-.368 (5.133)
Adjusted R2	.385	.316	.256

* $p < .05$, ** $p < .01$, *** $p < .001$

Note—The reference category for Topic is entertainment, for Media it is video

6.4 Network analysis

So far, the central claim of this essay reiterates the importance of a submitter's network for his stories' chances to trigger a global cascade. In particular, a submitter's friends (that is the mutual relationships) have proven to be of crucial importance in the propagation process. Further, I have shown that the distribution of success is highly skewed between successful submitters. Thus, it is of particular interest to analyze the interconnectedness between these very successful submitters. This would move control of content strongly towards a distinct group of individuals, for the following two reasons:

1) Submitters of the "top-group" are per se highly successful in submitting their own stories that become popular. This process is strongly influenced by the submitter's friends.
2) A high mutual connectedness would thus imply that these highly successful submitters also affect the chances of the other members of the top-group to get stories to the front page.

To analyze this I perform a network analysis (Hanneman 2005) of the 290 submitters that contributed the 846 popular stories (front page) between September 14th and 20th 2009. To form a basis of comparison, I split the group into two subgroups. Subgroup A consists of 120 users that have submitted one story each that later got promoted to front page. Subgroup B consists of the 119 users that have submitted 3 – 14 popular stories. I thus control for size of the networks by selecting similarly sized groups that are clearly distinguishable in terms of their success (number of popular stories). Thereby, I compare the different network measures shown in Table 21. The results clearly depict that the users in subgroup B show a much higher connectedness than the less successful users in subgroup A. The average degree centrality[21], for example, is a standard network measure, which takes into account the number of connections that incident with a node, i.e. how many ties a node has. For subgroup B this measure ends up being a remarkable seven times as large as for A (38.52 versus 5.53).

Average closeness centrality, which is regarded as a more sophisticated network measure, quantifies the distance of a node to all other nodes in the network measured with average shortest path length. That means, that the closer a node is to all other nodes, the easier information may reach it, the higher its closeness centrality.

---

21 Note that as I am only observing mutual friendship, indegree vs. outdegree centrality are no issue here, as they are the same.

Said in other words, degree closeness "can be regarded as a measure of how long it will take information to spread from a given vertex to others in the network" (Newman 2005, p.40). The average closeness centrality for subgroup A is 14 compared to 63.32 for B, which again shows that in subgroup B the individuals are on average much closer to one another. Degree and closeness centrality are based on the reach-ability of a node within a network.

Table 21: Network statistics for subnetworks A and B

Network measures	A	B
Number of Nodes	119	120
Number of mutual links	448	2810
Number of isolated Nodes	36	4
Avg. Degree Centrality	5.53	38.52
Avg. Betweenness Centrality	1.37	0.5
Avg. Closeness Centrality	14	63.32
Avg. Reach	46.16	93.42
Avg. Size of Network	929.24	3156.45

Note—Network A consists of users that submitted 1 popular story between Sept 14th – 20th. Subnetwork B consists of users that submitted 3 – 14 stories.

Another approach to centrality builds on the idea that that a person is more central if he or she is more important as an intermediary in the network. I therefore use "betweenness" as a third centrality measure. Betweenness is reflective of network centrality, i.e. it counts the shortest paths between pairs of nodes on a network that pass through a given node. Nodes with high betweenness sit on paths between many others and may thus have some influence over the spread of information across the network. In other words, the betweenness indicates the extent to which a person is needed as a link in the chain of contacts (Newmann 2005, de Rooy 2005). For the subgroup A this average betweenness is 1.37 (min (0), max (16.60), SD (2.50)) while for subgroup B it is 0.5 —(min (0), max (15.38), SD (1.79)), indicating the much higher importance of individual nodes for subgroup A in linking the network. Even though the maximum for both groups is similar, group A has 44 nodes with a betweenness > 1, while the same is true for only eleven individuals in group B.

A visual representation of the two subgroups and mutual connections between the nodes further clarifies this aspect (Figure 5 and 6). One can visually observe the less dense structure for subgroup A compared to B that has more than six times as many mutual links. Also observable is the difference in the number of isolated nodes (36 for A vs. 4 for B). This underlines the difference in a node's reach-ability between the two subgroups as expressed by degree and closeness centrality. Also, betweenness centrality becomes more obvious as subgroup A relies to a greater extent on specific individuals linking the group.

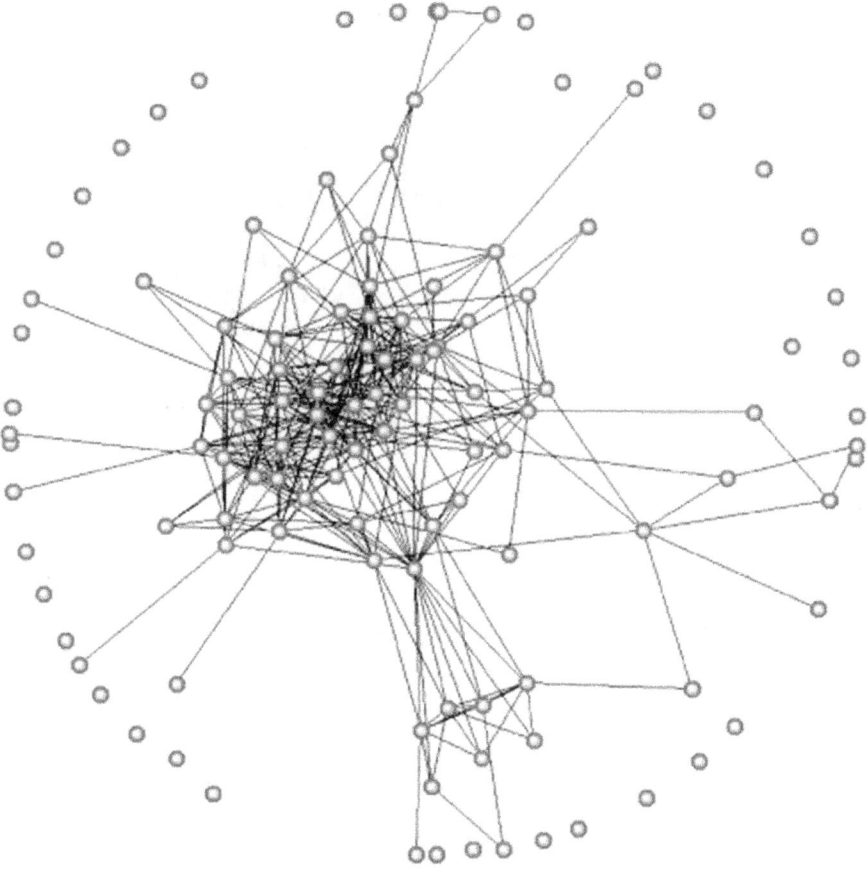

Figure 5: Subnetwork A (shows those 119 users that submitted 1 popular story)

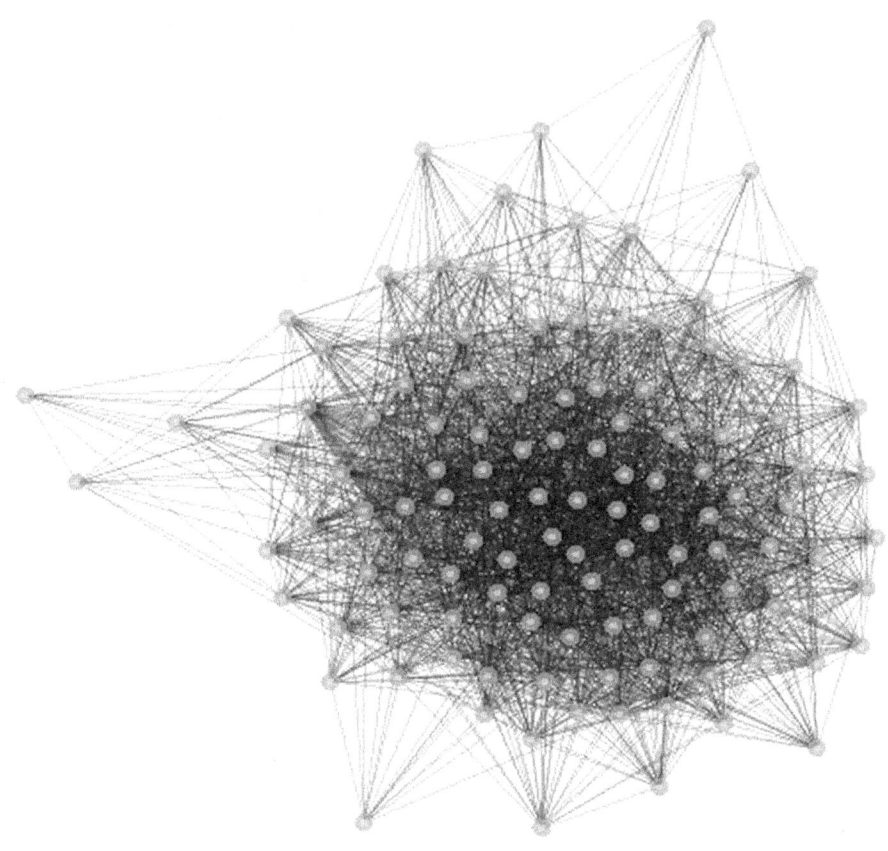

Figure 6: Subnetwork B (shows 120 users that submitted 3-14 popular stories)

7. Conclusions

7.1 Discussion of results

In this essay I examined factors that influence the popularity of User-generated Content, a common theme on the Internet and the Web 2.0. A widely circulated thesis suggests that "the wisdom of crowds" accounts for superior knowledge or quality of content in UGC-settings. One expectation of such a "participatory democracy" (Fuchs 2007) is that it distributes control of content between the users and therefore, breaks with traditional structures of editorial control. However, I posit that other factors are at work and that the information propagation process is largely affected (and in a way biased) by aspects of the submitter's network—which, at least in part, contradicts the aforementioned thesis.

Contrary to the idea of shared control of content I find that the distribution of the number of popular stories per user is highly skewed. For example, only 1% of submitters that managed to get at least one story to popular status controlled 50% of the popular stories over the course of three years. I further find strong support for my hypotheses that the size and structure of the submitter's egocentric social network appear to be the major drivers propagating a story through the local cascade into popularity status.

Upon examining the roles of different groups in social networks I find, somewhat contrary to the extant literature, evidence for the notion of the "strength of strong ties" in the local cascade phase. That is, even though both groups receive information in the same way, the "stronger" friends are more important than the "weaker" fans for the purpose of content promotion.

I use several approaches to control for content. Neither the content categories and media type, nor the automated content analysis show any considerable influence on the chances of a story to reach popularity. These findings have important implications, as they highlight the disproportionately influential role of a few individuals as they move content to exceed a threshold and become widely noticeable. For the marketing discipline, this seemingly implies that strong word of mouth might be triggered more easily just by virtue of better connected users initiating it.

With respect to the global cascade, which is a truer measure of success of propagation, I find support for the hypothesized and counterintuitive assertion that the influence of the network in the local stage of propagation on the global success of a story is actually inverted. More precisely, the higher the share of network votes bringing the content to the popular status during the local cascade, the lower the overall success tends to be. This implies that content that relies on the submitter's network to reach the global stage is of less interest to the public. However, the majoriy of popular content is triggered only by the network.

Additionally, the network analysis reveals that submitters who have higher hit rates are much more inter-connected than submitters with lower hit rates. This could fuel the notion of *the rich get richer* in this social networking environment. Thus, it is not only that successful submitters are per se successful in terms of submitting content that later becomes popular. They also have a indirect influence on popular stories as they vote on their friends stories.

The findings are consistent with my thesis on egocentric network's influence in propagation of information. Since global success is conditional on reaching popularity status (front page), and reaching front page is being aided by the network of the submitter, there is a concern that stories, which otherwise might find traction with the universe of all users are not reaching the front page and thus being denied visibility. This important insight also points to an inefficiency in information propagation on the Web 2.0 in general and on user controlled social news sites in particular and suggests a potential hindrance for UGC to have appropriate impact on a broader social scale. Or in other words, that the concept of wisdom of crowds may not work as well as it is often argued.

7.2 Limitations and future research

One aspect of limitation relating to the data is the fact that I cannot take into account the effect of "burials" i.e. stories that get buried from the site disappears from the site. This is a function on Digg, where users may vote content down that they consider inappropriate or wrong.

This is not readily accounted in the diggs (that is, a burial is not simply a deduction of one vote from the number of diggs) but is based upon a parallel, albeit undisclosed mechanism. A story gets buried if relative to the number of diggs a critical mass of users votes it down. As a cautionary note I state that, although this is an issue, it is not expected to have a large overall effect. There is also evidence that stories in this context tend to have a lower number of diggs. I reran the data collection 12 weeks after the initial data collection 6.8% of the total number of stories had disappeared. However, there was no popular story among these buried stories.

An empirical limitation relates to the fact that I do not conduct qualitative content analysis, as this would imply very large scale, subjective data coding of content. However, I conjecture that qualitative judgment of content is more likely to influence the overall success of global cascades. I consider this direction a rather promising approach, yet difficult to implement avenue for future research.

The network analysis reveals detailed connectedness of successful submitters. At this point, I am unable to identify and separate cause and effect. Is it popularity of stories by some submitters inducing connectedness or rather connectedness leading to more popularity of stories from these submitters? This leads to the connectedness aspect, that even though I underline the crucial importance of the submitter's network, I do not exactly know how these networks develop. This question is very worthy of future research as well.

Essay 2: How Social Networks Develop on the Web 2.0

1. Introduction

As argued in essay 1 of this dissertation, egocentric social networks play a crucial role in the functioning of social news sites. I have provided evidence that a submitter's network size and network structure are of superior importance for a story's chances to become popular. At the same time aspects of message and content seem to play a secondary role in the process of information dissemination. Users with large networks (and with a smaller proportion of friends compared to fans) tend to have better hit rates when it comes to the submission of stories that subsequently get promoted to the front page. Users with no or very small networks tend to have very little chance of their stories reaching the front page.

Obviously, network size is not distributed randomly between users but instead networks grow for some reason. As argued in essay 1, it is not assumed, that the social networks at Digg do largely consist of real-world acquaintances. Therefore the question arises what causes these networks to grow and why some users are so much more successful in generating friends and fans than others?

This essay shall be regarded as a conceptual work that offers some initial insights into how networks form in a Web 2.0-related context. In section 2 I discuss general assumption related to the utility of network formation from a game theoretic perspective. In section 3 I develop different hypotheses related to the source network I use in essay 1. I conclude in section 4. However, so far I have not been able to collect and transform the data necessary to empirically test the proposed hypotheses.

2. Utility of networks

Structurally network formation builds on cooperation. When two individuals decide to engage in a relationship—out of which networks evolve—they are willing to cooperate. Cooperation can be observed at many different levels of biological organization, from genes cooperating in genomes to the decisive organizing principles of human society, that form by far the most complex games of cooperation and defection (Nowak 2006). Lozano et al. (2008, p. 184) refer to the question of how cooperation emerges in human groups as "one of the most intriguing puzzles of modern science" and Axelrod (1982, p. 3) asks the question that "has intrigued people for a long time": Under what conditions will cooperation emerge in a world of egoists without central authority? Can cooperation be engendered more on the 'hidden' net, than in the real world, for the same set of people (who do not know each other a priori)?

For the evolution of cooperation, Nowak (2006) discusses five mechanisms: kin selection, direct reciprocity, indirect reciprocity, network reciprocity and group selection. For the purpose of explaining egocentric network formation, I subsequently build on direct reciprocity. Assume that each individual of a population has the options of either cooperating or defecting with the other individuals when it comes to the formation of egocentric networks. Thereby, the act of cooperating (that is befriending) implies the cost c for the cooperator and yields the benefit b for the other player.

Thereby, c is determined by the aspect that adding an individual to the personal network has the implication of being informed about all of the other user's subsequent actions. Given that the attention span is limited, each player only has a certain capacity of listening to other players. Thus, he needs to apply a cognitive effort to process each of the incoming information which results in c.[22]

The benefit b is determined by the fact that all the players that cooperate enlarge the network. As discussed in essay 1, the only way to display *status* on social news sites is by having large networks. Further, the size of the network positively influences the chances for popularity.

---

[22] Note that c enlarges the friend/fan (respectively friend/network) ratio. This is because every cooperation initiated by a user increases the number of friends and thus enlarges the ratio. As I have shown in essay 1, this ratio negatively affects chances for popularity, the broadest measure of success on social news sites, every player is assumed to strive for.

As we face the structure of repeated encounters, the befriended player may cooperate in a subsequent game (which means any time after the initial befriending), which would result in a benefit for the initiator. Partially following Nowak and May (1992), cooperating and defecting—in terms of adding friends or refusing to do so—results in the following game. Mutual cooperation gives both players a payoff of R. If a cooperator meets a defector, the latter receives the payoff T. The cooperator gets S. If both defect the payoff is P each.

The game is specified by imposing $T > R > P > S$. The payoffs have the values $T > 1$ ($b>1$, the defector receives the benefit of enlarging his network by one at no cost), $R=1$ ($b-c=1$, both players receive a benefit and both have costs), $P=0$ and $S<0$ ($c<0$, no benefits, only costs). Thus, the equilibrium is defection.

Table 22: Game 1

	Cooperate	Defect
Cooperate	R/R (1/1)	S/T (<0/>1)
Defect	T/S (>1/<0)	P/P (0/0)

Table 23: Game 2

	Cooperate	Defect
Cooperate	R/R (>1/>1)	S/T (0/>1)
Defect	T/S (>1/0)	P/P (0/0)

However, this should only be true for well established players with a significant network size. For new players that just joined the game and have zero or no significant network, I assume the payoffs to be different. With zero other users they listen to, new players are not exposed to any "noise", that is they do not get informed about any submissions etc. Therefore $c=0$ for cooperating and the main objective of such a user is to gain network size that is to find any other user that is willing to cooperate, be it mutual or not. Therefore $T = R > P = S$. The payoffs are $T>1$ ($b>1$), $R>1$ ($b-c>1$), P and $S=0$ ($c=0$) and the equilibrium is cooperation. However, the two games shown above incorporate the two endpoints of the continuum of network size, a new player with zero network and an established player with a large network.

For the purpose of analyzing the benefits and costs that result from the different relationships for all categories of players (all network sizes and configurations), the following specifications need to be applied. A user A can add other users to his network and subsequently gets informed about their actions. I call these users *friends* (x_i). Alternatively other users can add A to their network and subsequently get informed about all of A's actions. I call these users *fans* (y_i) of A. The relationship can also be mutual, that is if A has befriended B and B has befriended A. I call B a *mutual friend* of A (z_i) and vice versa[23]. The costs c—that result through the procession of information—for each user are expected to be a function of the number of users x_i, z_i the player has befriended (and therefore all users the player is listening to whether it is a mutual friendship or not).

When the player starts adding the first users to his network, I expect costs to be marginal and increase only slightly with each user added. This is because the stream of information generated by those few users is easy to handle and process. As the number of users increases further, the notifications about submissions, comments and diggs are expected to reach a point where the user needs to apply a high degree of cognitive effort to process all the incoming information. This is where $c(x,z)$ reaches its inflection point. After this point the user's capabilities of processing this information thoroughly are presumably exceeded and subsequent additions to his network are inducing decreasing marginal costs because he processes the incoming information partly selectively and in a superficial way. The higher the number of friends increases after this point, the lower the marginal costs of each user added, or in other words, after a certain point it doesn't make much of a difference if even more get added one is supposed to listen to.

---

[23] Note that the terminology used here varies from the one used in essay 1, as the perspective has been expanded

Thus, I expect the following cost function, derived from the above made assumptions.

$$c(x,z) = a/(1+e^{b-dx}) + a/(1+e^{b-dz}) \quad (1)$$

$$= a[2 + e^{-b}(e^{dx} + e^{dz})] \quad (2)$$

where a indicates the amplitude of the function (height), b the position on the x-axis and d the width of the function. I assume a, b and d to be identical for x_i and z_i.

The benefit $b^I(x)$ of adding the x_i to the network is to get informed about activity of individuals the respective user wants to listen to. This is related to the idea that the user gets informed about (upcoming) stories submitted by his friends. I assume this benefit to be

$$b^I(x) = \sum a_i x_i \quad (3)$$

where a_i is the individual benefit each user added generates.

Additionally, a different benefit is expected to be a function of users y_i, z_i that have befriended the player. As shown in essay 1, a growing egocentric network (that is all the others that are listening to a user—or in other words the fans/mutual friends) enhances the chances for submitting content that will later get promoted to the front page. Additionally, this is one of the few—and without doubt the most visible—ways to express status on a social news site[24].

As the marginal utility ($1/x$) for each additional fan/mutual friend decreases (but remains positive), I assume this benefit to follow the function

$$b^N(y) = ln(y) + n \quad (4)$$

$$b^N(z) = ln(z) + n \quad (5)$$

where n is the individual level of benefit that the first fan or mutual friend to add the player to his network generates. $ln(y)+n$, $ln(z)+n > 0$, as the benefit is always expected to be positive.

---

[24] Also, the number of popular stories or the number of diggs on the popular stories/per popular story could be considered an expression of status but these measures are far less obvious and would require a higher degree of involvement to assess.

3. Development of egocentric network

3.1 General network formation

Naturally, the question arises what users can do to enlarge their networks—or in other words to proactively develop fandom[25]. Of course one strategy is to befriend other users and hope for the befriended to respond and engage in a mutual friendship. This would enlarge the initiator's network by one. However, the above discussed cost function should generally prohibit such conduct on a large scale. Therefore, the preferred strategy should be to attract potential fans by other means than by first befriending them.

Out of the millions of registered users on a SNS it cannot be expected that a player chooses just about any user to play a game with if the later does not stick out of the mass. Instead, it is reasonable to argue that because of specific actions taken, others get interested in further actions and therefore add the respective users to their network. Apparently, this should mainly be driven by content that is widely visible and has reached a prominent position. A user striving to enlarge his network should therefore try to get as many stories to the front page as possible, as this enhances his chances that other players are willing to play a game with him, after noticing him.

> **H1**: Each significant increase in a user's network is (directly) preceded (12/24h) by content submitted by this user getting promoted to the front page.

In essay 1 I have shown that the influence of the personal network in terms of promoting the story from the local to the global stage is inverted. This means that the higher the share of friends and fans that voted on a story in the local cascade stage, the lower the overall number of votes in the global stage tends to be. I expect the same underlying factors detailed in the development of H4 of essay 1 to be at work when it comes to the formation of networks. When a story gets promoted to the front page that is of higher interest to the public (represented through a smaller share of promoters that belong to the submitter's network in the local cascade stage, see the development of H4 of essay 1), more unaligned users should be willing to play a game with the submitter of this content, resulting in a higher number of fans added to the network. Thus,

---

25 However, I assume this to be true only after the user has exceeded a certain network size and the costs of adding further friends/mutual friends are significant

H2: Conditional on a story reaching the global cascade phase, the larger (smaller) the share of the submitter's network promoting the story in the local cascade, the lower (greater) the number of users joining the submitter's network (as fans) in the first stage (12/24h) of the global cascade phase.

3.2 Initial stage

If the above described process explain network formation, the question remains, how individuals exceed the initial stage of their existence on a SNS. With initial stage I refer to the stage where the user has not yet gained any significant network and has therefore no significant chance to submit stories that later become popular.

Thus, for each user exceeding/overcoming this stage, other, exogenous processes should be at work, at least partially. More precisely, I expect the personal, "real-world" contacts of a user with no network to be the ones to first become fans of a user. Also mutual friends are of interest that initially were fans, i.e. the friends that initiated the cooperation. Of course, in a setting of a SNS, one cannot test if a connection between two users existed, before they befriended on Digg. However, the only logical explanation for the pattern described above is such a structure. Therefore, I assume that a user gains fans, even if he has not produced a notable action since his registration.

H3: Conditional on a user not having submitted a popular story, other users exist that become fans of him/her (and mutual friends that were initially fans).

It has to be noted that even though H3 seems somewhat obvious, no logical explanation exists that builds on processes that are endogenous to SNS.

3.3 Tie strength

In essay 1 I have distinguished between weak and strong ties of a submitter. I provided evidence that the latter have shown to be more influential when it comes to the promotion of content. However, I assume that even within the group of strong ties, differences in tie strength exist. One fundamental goal of human behavior is the "goal of affiliation". And one of the clearest implications of our desire to affiliate with others is that the more we like and approve of them, the more likely we are to take actions to cultivate close relationships with them (Cialdini and Goldstein 2004). Consistent with my remarks on homophily in section 4.2.2 of essay 1, this is expected to result in the fact that a higher interaction rate between two individuals in the preceding period is expected to result in a higher probability to promote each other's content today. Thus,

> **H4**: The higher the interaction rate between two users, the higher the probability to promote each other's content.

4. Conclusion

This conceptual essay aims to shed light onto the development of social networks in a Web 2.0 context. From a game theoretic perspective I provide arguments, why I assume cooperation to develop. The hypotheses developed in section three focus on the relationship between user actions (in terms of submissions) and network formation. These hypotheses could be tested empirically, however the respective data is not available at this point of time. In general, this short essay is supposed to serve as a thought-provoking impulse for future research.

References

Adanic, Lada A., E. Adar. 2003. Friends and neighbors on the Web. *Social Networks* 25 211-230.

Alexa. 2010. www.alexa.com, Information retrieved on Jan 11th 2010.

Anderson, Lisa R., C. A. Holt. 1997. Information cascades in the laboratory. *American Economic Review* 87(5) 847-862.

Arndt, J. 1967. Role of Product-Related Conversations in the Diffusion of a New Product. *Journal of Marketing Research* 4(3) 291-295.

Axelrod, Robert (1984): The Evolution of Cooperation. New York: Basic Books

Berger, Jonah, K. L. Milkman. 2010. Social Transmission and Viral Culture. Working Paper. The Wharton School, University of Pennsylvania.

Bikhchandani, Sushil, D. Hirshleifer, I. Welch. 1992. A theory of fads, fashion, custom, and cultural change as informational cascades. *Journal of Political Economy* 100(5) 992–1026.

Bret, Jeanne M., M. Olekalns, R. Friedman, N. Goates, C. Anderson, C. Lisco. 2007. Sticks and Stones: Language, Face, and Online Dispute Resolution. Academy of Management Journal. 50(1) 85-99.

Carley, Kathleen. 1991. A Theory of Group Stability. *American Sociological Review* 25(June) 331-54.

Chevalier, Judith A, D. Mayzlin. 2006. The Effect of Word of Mouth on Sales: Online Book Reviews. *Journal of Marketing Research* 43(3) 345-54.

Cialdini, Robert B.; N. Goldstein. 2004. Social Influence: Compliance and Conformity, in: Annual Review of Psychology. 55. 591-621.

Clary, E. Gil, M. Snyder, R. Ridge, J. Copeland, A. Stukas, J. Haugen, P. Miene.1998. Understanding and assessing the motivations of volunteers: A functional approach. *Journal of Personality and Social Psychology*. 74. 1516-1530

Cooke, Mike, N. Buckley. 2008. Web 2.0, social networks and the future of market research. *International Journal of Market Research* 50(2) 267-292.

Cox, David R. 1972. Regression models and life-tables (with discussion). *Journal of the Royal Statistical Society*. B 34 187-220.

Cox, David R.; D. Oakes. 1984. Analysis of Survival Data. *Monographs on Statistics and Applied Probability*. 21. Chapman & Hall. London.

De Rooy, W., A. Mrvar, V. Batagelj. 2005. *Exploratory Social Network Analysis with Pajek*. Cambridge University Press, New York.

Feik, Lawrence F., L. Price. 1987. The Market Maven: A Diffuser of Marketplace Information. *Journal of Marketing* 51(1) 83-97.

Fivush, Robyn, K. Marin, M. Crawford, M. Reynolds, C. R. Brewin. 2007. Children's narratives and well-being. Cognition and Emotion. 21(7). 1414-1434.

Frenzen, Jonathan, K. Nakamoto. 1993. Structure, Cooperation, and the Flow of Market Information. *Journal of Consumer Research* 20(3) 360-375.

Fuchs, Christian. 2007. Internet and Society: Social Theory in the Information Age.

Godes, David, D. Mayzlin. 2004. Using Online Conversations to Study Word-of-Mouth Communication. Marketing Science 23(4) 545-60.

Goldenberg, J., S. Han, D. R. Lehmann, J. W. Hong. 2009. The Role of Hubs in the Adoption Process. Journal of Marketing. 73(2) 1-13.

Granovetter, Mark S. 1973. The Strength of Weak Ties. *American Journal of Sociology* 78(6) 1360-1380.

Granovetter, Mark S. 1982. The Strength of Weak Ties: A Network Theory Revisited. Marsden, Peter V., N. Lin, eds. *Social Structure and Network Analysis*. Beverly Hills: Sage 105-130.

Hanneman, R. A. 2005. Introduction to Social Network Methods, online book, University of California, Riverside.

Horowitz, Adam, M. Athitakis, M. Laswell, O. Thomas. 2005. 101 Dumbest Moments in Business. *Business 2.0* 1(January).

Huang, Jen-Hung, Y.-F. Chen. 2006. Herding in Online Product Choice. *Psychology & Marketing* 23(5) 413-28.

Humphreys, Ashlee. 2010. Megamarketing: The Creation of Markets as a Social Process. Journal of Marketing. 74(March).1-19.

Kalbfleisch, John D.; Ross L. Prentice. 2002. The Statistical Analysis of Failure Time Data. Second Edition. John Wiley & Sons. Hoboken, New Jersey

Kaplan, E.L.; P. Meier. 1958. Nonparametric estimation from incomplete observations. Journal of the American Statistical Society 53 457-481.

Katz, Elihu. 1957. The Two-Step Flow of Communication: An Up-To-Date Report on a Hypothesis. *The Public Opinion Quarterly* 21(1) 61-78.

Katz, Elihu, P.-F. Lazarsfeld. 1955. Personal Influence: the Part Played by People in the Flow of Mass Communications. Glencoe, IL: Free Press.

Kornish, Laura J. 2009. Are User Reviews Systematically Manipulated? Evidence from the Helpfulness Ratings. Working Paper. University of Colorado.

Lazarfeld, Paul Felix, R. K. Merton. 1954. Friendship as a Social Process: A Substantive and Methodological Analysis. Berger, M., T. Abel, C. Page, eds. *Freedom and Control in Modern Society*. Van Nostrand: New York.

Lozano, Serqi, A. Arenas, A. Sánchez. 2008. Community connectivity and heterogeneity: Clues and Insights on Cooperation on Social Networks. *Journal of Economic Interaction and Coordination*. 3. 183–199.

Mayzlin, Diana. 2006. Promotional Chat on the Internet. *Marketing Science* 25(2) 155-63.

McPherson, Miller, L. Smith-Lovin, J. M. Cook. 2001. Birds of a Feather: Homophily in Social Networks. *Annual Review of Sociology* 27(1) 415-44.

Musser, John; T. O'Reilly. 2006. Web 2.0, Principles and Best Practices. O'ReillyRadar. http://oreilly.com/catalog/web2report/chapter/web20_report_excerpt.pdf (retrieved Mar 17 2010)

Newmann, M. E. J. 2005. A measure of betweenness centrality based on random walks. *Social Networks*. 27(1) 39-54.

Nov, Oded. 2007. What Motivates Wikipedians? *Communications of the ACM*. 50(11) 60-64.

Nowak, Martin A. 2006. Five Rules for the Evolution of Cooperation. *Science*. 314. 1560-63.

Nowak, Martin A., R. May. 1992. Evolutionary games and spatial chaos. *Nature*. 359. 826-829.

Nielsen Netrating. 2006. User-generated content drives half of U.S. top 10 fastest growing Web brands. http://www.nielsen-online.com/pr/PR_060810.PDF.

O'Brien, Keith. 2004. Kryptonite's response to lock controversy doesn't satisfy bloggers. *PRweek* (US) Vol 7.

Pennebaker, James W., C. K. Chung. 2009. Computerized Text Analysis of Al-Qaeda Transcripts, in: Krippendorff, Klaus, M. A. Bock. 2009. *The Content Analysis Reader*. Sage. 453-465.

Pennebaker, James W.; Chung, Cindy K.; Ireland, Molly; Gonzales, Amy; Booth, Joger J. (2007): The Development and Psychometric Properties of LIWC2007, LIWC.net, Austin, Texas.

Perlmutter, David D., M. McDaniel. 2005. The Ascent of Blogging. *Nieman Reports*. 59(3) 60-64.

Pisani, Francis. 2006. Journalism and Web 2.0. *Nieman Reports*. 60(4) 42-44.

Polgreen, Lydai. 2004. A Ballpoint Trick Infuriates Bicyclists. *The New York Times*, Late Edition (East Coast), Sept 17th 2004, p. B1.

Senecal, Sylvain, J. Nantel. 2004. The influence of online product recommendations on Consumers' Online Choices. *Journal of Retailing* 80(1) 159-69.

Shannon, Victoria. 2006. A 'more revolutionary' Web. *The New York Times*, Online Edition, Mar 23, 2006.

www.nytimes.com/2006/05/23/technology/23iht-web.html (retrieved Mar 17, 2010)

Smith, Tom. 2009. The Social Media Revolution. *International Journal of Market Research.* 51(4) 559-561.

Smith, Peter J. 2002. Analysis of Failure and Survival Data. Chapman & Hall. London

Sorkin, Andrew Ross. 2006. Dot-Com Boom Echoed in Deal to Buy YouTube. *New York Times*, Late Edition (East Coast), Oct 10th 2006, p. A1.

Surowiecki, James. 2004. The Wisdom of Crowds: Why the Many Are Smarter Than the Few and How Collective Wisdom Shapes Business, Economics, Societies and Nations. Bantam Dell Publishers

Van den Bulte, Christophe, S. Wuyts. 2007. Social Networks and Marketing. Cambridge, MA: Marketing Science Institute.

Van Dijck, José. 2009. Users like you? Theorizing agency in user-generated content. Media, *Culture & Society.* 31(1) 41-58.

Waldman, Simon. 2005. Arriving at the Digital News Age. *Nieman Reports* 59(1) 78 - 79.

Watts, Duncan J., P. S. Dodds. 2007. Influentials, Networks, and Public Opinion Formation. *Journal of Consumer Research* 34(4) 441-458.

Appendices

Appendix 1: Data collection and transformation

For purposes of data collection the Application Programming Interface (API) of Digg was used. APIs generally serve the purpose to return data of the respective site in a format that can more easily be integrated into websites or databases. The Digg API accepts REST (Representational State Transfers) requests and offers several response types: XML, JSON, Javascript, and serialized PHP. In addition, a PEAR module is available for PHP as well other open-source toolkits. I used the XML response format. Exemplary requests and responses for stories, diggs and fan information are stated below (all dates are given in Unix time)[26].

Request for the two most recently submitted stories (request timestamp 1269004081):

http://services.digg.com/stories?count=2&appkey=http://test.com

Response (in xml):
<?xml version="1.0" encoding="UTF-8"?>
*<stories timestamp="1269004081" min_date="1266412080" total="564848" offset="0" count="2"> <story link="http://online.wsj.com/article/SB10001424052748703976804575114151637806636.html?mod=wsj_share_digg" submit_date="1269004073" diggs="1" id="20031980" comments="0" href="http://digg.com/political_opinion/WSJ_com_Opinion_Obama_s_3_000_0 00_000_000_*
Tax_Hike" status="upcoming" media="news">
  <description>President Obama has offered a budget that does nothing to address the nation's serious short-term and long-term fiscal problems--and indeed makes them worse. By doubling the national debt above pre-recession levels</description>
  <title>WSJ.com - Opinion: Obama's $3,000,000,000,000 Tax Hike</title>

---

[26] Note that more requests were used during the course of the analysis, i.e. request for friends and comments. If applicable, mutuality in friend or fan output is indicated through the additional variable "mutual", where "1" indicates mutuality of the relationship

```xml
<user name="eslaugh" registered="1258969775" profileviews="135" icon="http://digg.com/users/eslaugh/l.png"/>
 <topic name="Political Opinion" short_name="political_opinion"/>
 <container name="World &amp; Business" short_name="world_business"/>
 <shorturl short_url="http://digg.com/d31M3ES" view_count="0"/>
</story>
<story link="http://www.noromor.com/2010/03/19/web-com-ph-hosting-review-in-the-philippines/" submit_date="1269004065" diggs="1" id="20031979" comments="0" href="http://digg.com/hardware/Web_com_ph_Hosting_Review_in_the_Philippines" status="upcoming" media="news">
 <description>A review of web hosting service in the Philippines offered by Web.com.ph</description>
 <title>Web.com.ph - Hosting Review in the Philippines</title>
 <user name="chardsnet" registered="1228931465" profileviews="241" fullname="Richard Noromor" icon="http://digg.com/users/chardsnet/l.png"/>
 <topic name="Hardware" short_name="hardware"/>
 <container name="Technology" short_name="technology"/>
 <thumbnail originalwidth="576" originalheight="1033" content-Type="image/jpeg" src="http://digg.com/hardware/Web_com_ph_Hosting_Review_in_the_Philippines/t.jpg" width="80" height="80"/>
 <shorturl short_url="http://digg.com/d31M3ER" view_count="0"/>
</story>
</stories>
```

Request for the 20 most recent diggs on story id 20008833 (request time 1269006144)

http://services.digg.com/story/20008833/diggs?count=20&appkey=http://test.com

Response (in xml):
```xml
<?xml version="1.0" encoding="UTF-8"?>
<events timestamp="1269006144" total="150" offset="0" count="20">
 <digg date="1269005956" story="20008833" id="274601224" user="stackolee" status="popular"/>
 <digg date="1269005781" story="20008833" id="274600714" user="maximilliontee" status="popular"/>
```

```xml
<digg date="1269005758" story="20008833" id="274600661" user="Hayley3AM" status="popular"/>
<digg date="1269005745" story="20008833" id="274600615" user="annjay" status="popular"/>
<digg date="1269005726" story="20008833" id="274600562" user="amoirae" status="popular"/>
<digg date="1269005723" story="20008833" id="274600551" user="misterteenwolf" status="popular"/>
<digg date="1269005695" story="20008833" id="274600475" user="shaunmdison1" status="popular"/>
<digg date="1269005678" story="20008833" id="274600417" user="Squiggimon" status="popular"/>
<digg date="1269005612" story="20008833" id="274600212" user="Elsewhere42" status="popular"/>
<digg date="1269005543" story="20008833" id="274600035" user="JesseUnruh" status="popular"/>
<digg date="1269005429" story="20008833" id="274599766" user="Iscariotpunk" status="popular"/>
<digg date="1269005399" story="20008833" id="274599704" user="jsmith39" status="popular"/>
<digg date="1269005368" story="20008833" id="274599644" user="moriarty23" status="popular"/>
<digg date="1269005338" story="20008833" id="274599559" user="upnorthgirl" status="popular"/>
<digg date="1269005335" story="20008833" id="274599552" user="thegman3" status="popular"/>
<digg date="1269005258" story="20008833" id="274599363" user="mebbin" status="popular"/>
<digg date="1269005255" story="20008833" id="274599356" user="Curiomime" status="popular"/>
<digg date="1269005252" story="20008833" id="274599352" user="DamonDD" status="popular"/>
<digg date="1269005179" story="20008833" id="274599196" user="benzylene" status="popular"/>
<digg date="1269005161" story="20008833" id="274599151" user="Batfishy" status="popular"/>
</events>
```

Request for the first 20 fans in alphabetical order of user UPick

http://services.digg.com/user/upick/fans?count=20&appkey=http://test.com

Response (in xml):
<?xml version="1.0" encoding="UTF-8"?>
<users timestamp="1269007098" total="7059" offset="0" count="20">
<user name="02nl" registered="1255917454" profileviews="582" icon="http://digg.com/img/udl.png" date="1258522801"/>
<user name="03cranec" registered="1254272763" profileviews="117" fullname="Chris" icon="http://digg.com/users/03cranec/l.png" date="1254438575"/>
<user name="03shane12" registered="1212551196" profileviews="1208" icon="http://digg.com/users/03shane12/l.png" date="1212893889"/>
<user name="0suitable0" registered="1233647199" profileviews="530" fullname="Andrew Birkholz" icon="http://digg.com/users/0suitable0/l.png" date="1234517588"/>
<user name="100artwork" registered="1220882470" profileviews="2260" icon="http://digg.com/users/100artwork/l.png" date="1220943827"/>
<user name="101dotcom" registered="1226589819" profileviews="1386" icon="http://digg.com/users/101dotcom/l.png" date="1226730559"/>
<user name="101lourdes" registered="1258387621" profileviews="265" fullname="Lourdes Witt" icon="http://digg.com/users/101lourdes/l.png" date="1264273425"/>
<user name="101Magazine" registered="1241108679" profileviews="330" fullname="Jonathan" icon="http://digg.com/users/101Magazine/l.png" date="1241109853"/>
<user name="111Toxicity111" registered="1211965862" profileviews="2465" fullname="Ashish Jain" icon="http://digg.com/users/111Toxicity111/l.png" date="1218786333"/>
<user name="11Christine" registered="1214272712" profileviews="4170" fullname="Christine " icon="http://digg.com/users/11Christine/l.png" date="1215055583"/>
<user name="11MK11" registered="1234128979" profileviews="33" fullname="Martin King" icon="http://digg.com/users/11MK11/l.png" date="1234132735"/>

\<user name="11ssims" registered="1196778918" profileviews="477" fullname="Sean Sims" icon="http://digg.com/users/11ssims/l.png" date="1218789123"/>
\<user name="123awang" registered="1227443783" profileviews="199" fullname="awang satrijana" icon="http://digg.com/users/123awang/l.png" date="1238331127"/>
\<user name="12thManBlog" registered="1250474114" profileviews="637" fullname="The12thMan" icon="http://digg.com/users/12thManBlog/l.png" date="1256782471"/>
\<user name="1418" registered="1225159484" profileviews="2025" fullname="Ahyat Ladibi" icon="http://digg.com/users/1418/l.png" date="1225177223"/>
\<user name="1618" registered="1203068401" profileviews="558" icon="http://digg.com/users/1618/l.png" date="1243951315"/>
\<user name="1776" registered="1185595763" profileviews="5825" fullname="Add me or the terrorists win!" icon="http://digg.com/users/1776/l.png" date="1259453312"/>
\<user name="1984USA" registered="1233071182" profileviews="1314" fullname="Winston Smith" icon="http://digg.com/users/1984USA/l.png" date="1238895245"/>
\<user name="19thkiller" registered="1203596477" profileviews="1150" fullname="aboo gaop" icon="http://digg.com/users/19thkiller/l.png" date="1224753128"/>
\<user name="1ADAM9" registered="1244393229" profileviews="437" fullname="Adam Smith" icon="http://digg.com/users/1ADAM9/l.png" date="1244889253"/> \</users>

As the maximum output per data call is restricted to 100 data points (that is "count" <= 100), the offset command needed to be applied to collect complete datasets. Initially, I used MS Excel 2007 and VBA macros to collect the data and perform the first transformations in MS Access 2007 (as described below). At a later point data collection was migrated to a custom software.

Data transformation

In the following I briefly describe the steps of data transformation that were necessary to get the appropriate measures.

1) Time-related specification of individual diggs: The Digg API does not specify in which phase a user dugg a story. However, for the course of analyses it was crucial to have this information available to be able to see who voted a story to the front page, i.e. attribute the status of a story to each digg. To be able to relate the diggs to the different phases of the promotion process (i.e. upcoming and popular stage), I used promotion time of a story. By filtering out the diggs a story received after promotion I was able to distinguish diggs during the upcoming stage from diggs during the popular stage for all stories that got promoted to the front page.

2) Transformation of networks: The central focus of this essay is the investigation of the influence of submitters' social networks on the popularity of the submitted stories. For the data to meet my definition of friends and fans, I needed to filter out the mutual friends and exclude mutual fans, as defined by Digg. I further needed to manipulate the network information such that only these individuals were considered that belonged to the submitter's network at time of submission.
I achieved this through the application of an individual time filter for each story such that only such individuals were considered where the befriending date was smaller than the submission date of the story. Additionally I filtered out inactive users whose profile had been deactivated or deleted. The sum of all mutual friendships for all submitters in the main period of analyses amounted to 369,042 and 1,085,386 for unidirectional fan-relationships.

3) Network-related specification of individual diggs: For the purpose of measuring the voting behavior of *friends* and *fans*, I further needed to determine for each digg a story received (during the upcoming and popular stage) if it was generated by a network member of the submitter that belonged to this network at time of submission. I achieved this through the comparison of the digging and the network information, taking into account the different time-related filters.

Appendix 2: Additional figures and tables

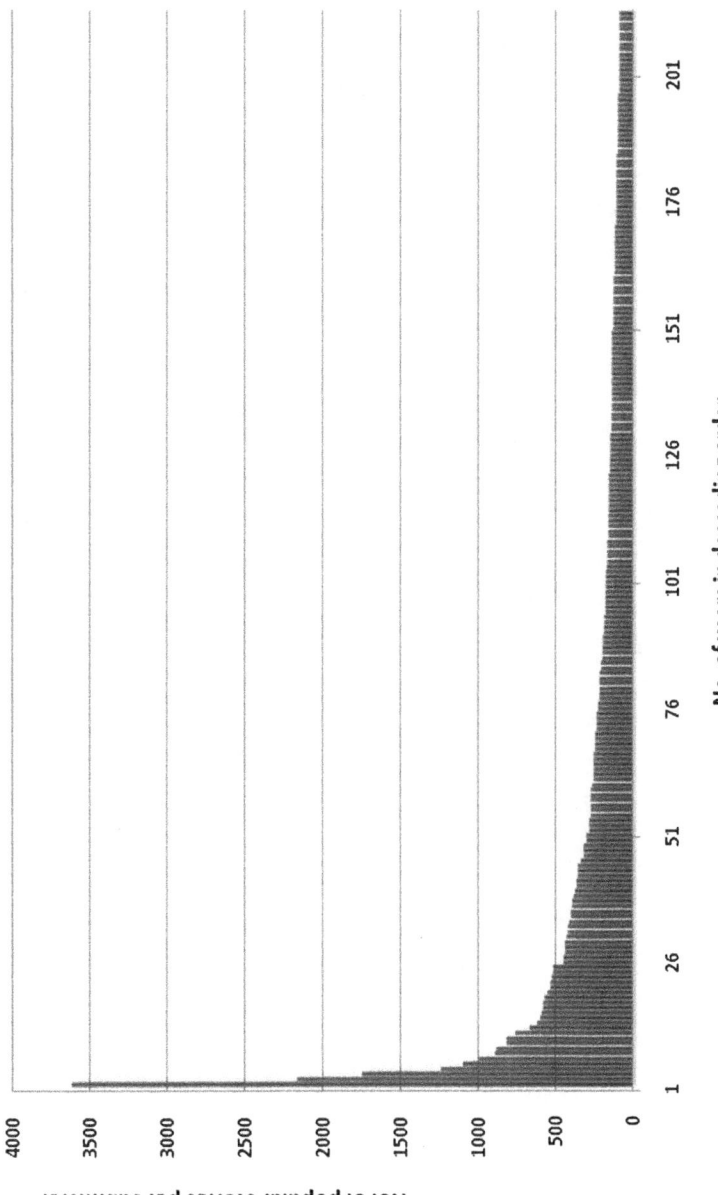

Figure 7: Number of popular stories per user.
(Note--Displayed are the 212 users that submitted 50% of the popular stories

Table 24: Results of models 7a – 9a

Variable		Model 7a	Model 8a	Model 9a
Network dummy 1 (1-81)		2.223 (.525)***	2.399 (.525)***	2.424 (.525)***
Network dummy 2 (82-687)		5.853 (.506)***	6.371 (.508)***	6.459 (.509)***
Network dummy 3 (688-1293)		6.868 (.512)***	7.049 (.512)***	7.066 (.513)***
Network dummy 4 (1294-max)		7.053 (.508)***	7.174 (.508)***	7.176 (.509)***
ratio Friends/Fans			-.410 (.076)***	-.397 (.074)***
DiggsCountUpcoming		.015 (.001)***	.014 (.001)***	.013 (.001)***
Topic	Gaming			.006 (.190)
(ref. cat. =	Lifestyle			-.080 (.130)
Entertainment)	Offbeat			-.135 (.132)
	Science			.499 (.134)***
	Sports			-.051 (.170)
	Technology			.122 (.128)
	World&Business			-.594 (.139)***
Media	Images			-.193 (.113)
(ref. cat. =	News			.143 (.135)
Video)				
-2LL		14264.933	14160.115	14075.557
-2LL null model	19626.612			

* $p < .05$, ** $p < .01$, *** $p < .001$

Table 25: Results of models 7b – 9b

Variable		Model 7b	Model 8b	Model 9b
Network dummy 1 (1-81)		2.226 (.525)***	2.383 (.525)***	2.403 (.525)***
Network dummy 2 (82-687)		5.819 (.506)***	6.283 (.508)***	6.330 (.509)***
Network dummy 3 (688-1293)		6.270 (.516)***	6.468 (.516)***	6.449 (.518)***
Network dummy 4 (1294-max)		6.617 (.511)***	6.768 (.511)***	6.761 (.511)***
ratio Friends/Fans			-.333 (.068)***	-.329 (.067)***
DiggsCountUpcoming		.004 (.001)***	.003 (.001)***	.003 (.001)**
Topic	Gaming			.230 (.190)
(ref. cat. =	Lifestyle			.010 (.130)
Entertainment)	Offbeat			-.037 (.132)
	Science			.385 (.134)**
	Sports			-.004 (.170)
	Technology			.170 (.128)
	World&Business			-.307 (.140)*
Media	Images			.021 (.135)
(ref. cat. =	News			-.275 (.112)
Video)				
Past hit rate		4.054 (.171)***	3.948 (.170)***	3.806 (.173)***
-2LL		13783.843	13696.581	13655.185
-2LL null model	19626.612			

* $p < .05$, ** $p < .01$, *** $p < .001$

Table 26: Results of models 13a – 15a

Variable		Model 13a	Model 14a	Model 15a
Network dummy 1 (1-81)		2.234 (.525)***	2.417 (.525)***	2.442 (.525)***
Network dummy 2 (82-687)		5.965 (.506)***	6.536 (.508)***	6.614 (.508)***
Network dummy 3 (688-1293)		7.218 (.511)***	7.396 (.511)***	7.422 (.512)***
Network dummy 4 (1294-max)		7.535 (.507)***	7.631 (.507)***	7.634 (.507)***
ratio Friends/Fans			-.452 (.078)***	-.434 (.075)***
DiggsFriendsUpcoming		.022 (.001)***	.020 (.001)***	.018 (.001)***
Topic	Gaming			.011 (.190)
(ref. cat. =	Lifestyle			-.046 (.130)
Entertainment)	Offbeat			-.107 (.131)
	Science			.510 (.134)***
	Sports			.009 (.170)
	Technology			.162 (.128)
	World&Business			-.595 (.140)***
Media	Images			.220 (.134)
(ref. cat. =	News			-.234 (.112)*
Video)				
-2LL		14426.612	14304.848	14207.712
-2LL null model	19626.612			

* $p < .05$, ** $p < .01$, *** $p < .001$

Table 27: Results of models 13b – 15b

Variable		Model 13b	Model 14b	Model 15b
Network dummy 1 (1-81)		2.226 (.525)***	2.388 (.525)***	2.412 (.525)***
Network dummy 2 (82-687)		5.889 (.506)***	6.370 (.508)***	6.437 (.509)***
Network dummy 3 (688-1293)		6.611 (.514)***	6.782 (.515)***	6.780 (.516)***
Network dummy 4 (1294-max)		7.000 (.509)***	7.118 (.509)***	7.122 (.509)***
ratio Friends/Fans			-.351 (.069)***	-.349 (.068)***
DiggsFriendsUpcoming		-.004 (.002)**	-.005 (.002)**	-.005 (.002)**
Topic	Gaming			.197 (.190)
(ref. cat. =	Lifestyle			.018 (.130)
Entertainment)	Offbeat			-.036 (.132)
	Science			.328 (.134)*
	Sports			.045 (.170)
	Technology			.178 (.128)
	World&Business			-.375 (.141)
Media	Images			.008 (.136)**
(ref. cat. =	News			-.280 (.112)*
Video)				
Past hit rate		4.615 (.162)***	4.482 (.160)***	4.327 (.164)***
-2LL		13796.260	13700.739	13656.645
-2LL null model	19626.612			

* $p < .05$, ** $p < .01$, *** $p < .001$

Table 28: Results of models 16a – 18a

Variable		Model 16a	Model 17a	Model 18a
Network dummy 1 (1-81)		2.235 (.525)***	2.424 (.525)***	2.455 (.525)***
Network dummy 2 (82-687)		6.034 (.506)***	6.637 (.507)***	6.753 (.508)***
Network dummy 3 (688-1293)		7.655 (.509)***	7.837 (.509)***	7.903 (.510)***
Network dummy 4 (1294-max)		8.049 (.505)***	8.131 (.506)***	8.134 (.506)***
ratio Friends/Fans			-.483 (.079)***	-.468 (.077)***
DiggsFansUpcoming		.037 (.005)***	.033 (.005)***	.025 (.005)***
Topic	Gaming			-.073 (.191)
(ref. cat. =	Lifestyle			-.033 (.130)
Entertainment)	Offbeat			-.102 (.131)
	Science			.504 (.134)***
	Sports			.061 (.170)
	Technology			.165 (.129)
	World&Business			-.782 (.139)***
Media	Images			.259 (.134)
(ref. cat. =	News			-.193 (.112)
Video)				
-2LL		14617.298	14482.329	14348.159
-2LL null model	19626.612			

* $p < .05$, ** $p < .01$, *** $p < .001$

Table 29: Results of models 16b – 18b

Variable		Model 16b	Model 17b	Model 18b
Network dummy 1 (1-81)		2.226 (.525)***	2.392 (.525)***	2.416 (.525)***
Network dummy 2 (82-687)		5.884 (.506)***	6.376 (.508)***	6.443 (.509)***
Network dummy 3 (688-1293)		6.640 (.513)***	6.815 (.513)***	6.812 (.514)***
Network dummy 4 (1294-max)		7.133 (.508)***	7.256 (.508)***	7.268 (.509)***
ratio Friends/Fans			-.369 (.071)***	-.366 (.070)***
DiggsFansUpcoming		-.031 (.005)***	-.033 (.005)***	-.036 (.006)***
Topic	Gaming			.201 (.191)
(ref. cat. =	Lifestyle			.015 (.130)
Entertainment)	Offbeat			-.069 (.132)
	Science			.348 (.134)**
	Sports			.116 (.171)
	Technology			.130 (.128)
	World&Business			-.392 (.140)**
Media	Images			.001 (.136)
(ref. cat. =	News			-.304 (.112)**
Video)				
Past hit rate		4.723 (.148)***	4.573 (.146)***	4.431 (.152)***
-2LL		13768.076	13670.330	13670.330
-2LL null model	19626.612			

* $p < .05$, ** $p < .01$, *** $p < .001$

Table 30: LIWC 2007 Categories

Category	Abbrev	Examples	Words in category	Validity (judges)
Linguistic Processes				
Word count	wc			
words/sentence	wps			
Dictionary words	dic			
Words>6 letters	sixltr			
Total function words	funct		464	.97/.40
Total pronouns	pronoun	I, them, itself	116	.91/.38
Personal pronouns	ppron	I, them, her	70	.88/.20
1st pers singular	i	I, me, mine	12	.62/.44
1st pers plural	we	We, us, our	12	.66/.47
2nd person	you	You, your, thou	20	.73/.34
3rd pers singular	shehe	She, her, him	17	.75/.52
3rd pers plural	they	They, their, they'd	10	.50/.36
Impersonal pronouns	ipron	It, it's, those	46	.78/.46
Articles	article	A, an, the	3	.14/.14
[Common verbs][a]	verb	Walk, went, see	383	.97/.42
Auxiliary verbs	auxverb	Am, will, have	144	.91/.23
Past tense [a]	past	Went, ran, had	145	.94/.75
Present tense [a]	present	Is, does, hear	169	.91/.74
Future tense [a]	future	Will, gonna	48	.75/.02
Adverbs	adverb	Very, really, quickly	69	.84/.48
Prepositions	prep	To, with, above	60	.88/.35
Conjunctions	conj	And, but, whereas	28	.70/.21
Negations	negate	No, not, never	57	.80/.28
Quantifiers	quant	Few, many, much	89	.88/.12
Numbers	number	Second, thousand	34	.87/.61
Swear words	swear	Damn, piss, fuck	53	.65/.48
Psychological Processes				
Social processes [b]	social	Mate, talk, they, child	455	.97/.59

Family	family	Daughter, husband, aunt	64	.81/.65
Friends	friend	Buddy, friend, neighbor	37	.53/.12
Humans	human	Adult, baby, boy	61	.86/.26
Affective processes	affect	Happy, cried, abandon	915	.97/.36
Positive emotion	posemo	Love, nice, sweet	406	.97/.40
Negative emotion	negemo	Hurt, ugly, nasty	499	.97/.61
Anxiety	anx	Worried, fearful, nervous	91	.89/.33
Anger	anger	Hate, kill, annoyed	184	.92/.55
Sadness	sad	Crying, grief, sad	101	.91/.45
Cognitive processes	cogmech	cause, know, ought	730	.97/.37
Insight	insight	think, know, consider	195	.94/.51
Causation	cause	because, effect, hence	108	.88/.26
Discrepancy	discrep	should, would, could	76	.80/.28
Tentative	tentat	maybe, perhaps, guess	155	.87/.13
Certainty	certain	always, never	83	.85/.29
Inhibition	inhib	block, constrain, stop	111	.91/.20
Inclusive	incl	And, with, include	18	.66/.32
Exclusive	excl	But, without, exclude	17	.67/.47
Perceptual processes [c]	percept	Observing, heard, feeling	273	.96/.43
See	see	View, saw, seen	72	.90/.43
Hear	hear	Listen, hearing	51	.89/.37
Feel	feel	Feels, touch	75	.88/.26
Biological processes	bio	Eat, blood, pain	567	.95/.53
Body	body	Cheek, hands, spit	180	.93/.45
Health	health	Clinic, flu, pill	236	.85/.38
Sexual	sexual	Horny, love, incest	96	.69/.34
Ingestion	ingest	Dish, eat, pizza	111	.86/.68
Relativity	relativ	Area, bend, exit, stop	638	.98/.51
Motion	motion	Arrive, car, go	168	.96/.41
Space	space	Down, in, thin	220	.96/.44
Time	time	End, until, season	239	.94/.58

Personal Concerns				
Work	work	Job, majors, xerox	327	.91/.69
Achievement	achieve	Earn, hero, win	186	.93/.37
Leisure	leisure	Cook, chat, movie	229	.88/.50
Home	home	Apartment, kitchen, family	93	.81/.57
Money	money	Audit, cash, owe	173	.90/.53
Religion	relig	Altar, church, mosque	159	.91/.53
Death	death	Bury, coffin, kill	62	.86/.40
Spoken categories				
Assent	assent	Agree, OK, yes	30	.59/.41
Nonfluencies	nonflu	Er, hm, umm	8	.28/.23
Fillers	filler	Blah, Imean, youknow	9	.63/.18

"Words in category" refers to the number of different dictionary words that make up the variable category. "Alphas" refer to the Cronbach alphas for the internal reliability of the specific words within each category. The binary alphas are computed on the occurrence/nonoccurrence of each dictionary word whereas the raw or uncorrected alphas are based on the percentage of use of each of the category words within the texts. All alphas were computed on a sample of 2800 randomly selected text files from our language corpus.

The LIWC dictionary generally arranges categories hierachically. For example, all pronouns are included in the overarching category of function words. The category of pronouns is the sum of personal and impersonal pronouns. There are some exceptions to the hierarchy rules:

[a] Common verbs are not included in the function word category. Similarly, common verbs (as opposed to auxiliary verbs) that are tagged by verb tense are included in the past, present, and future tense categories but not in the overall function word categories.

[b] Social processes include a large group of words (originally used in LIWC2001) that denote social processes, including all non-first-person-singular personal pronouns as well as verbs that suggest human interaction (talking, sharing).

[c] Perceptual processes include the entire dictionary of the Qualia category (which is a separate dictionary), which includes multiple sensory and perceptual dimensions associated with the five senses.

Table 31: Eigenvalues and rotation sums of squared loadings

Components	Initial Eigenvalues			Rotation Sums of Squared		
	Total	% of	Cumulative	Total	% of	Cumulative
1	9.007	13.245	13.245	4.587	6.745	6.745
2	3.477	5.114	18.359	3.121	4.590	11.335
3	2.752	4.046	22.405	3.023	4.446	15.780
4	2.384	3.506	25.911	2.779	4.086	19.866
5	2.252	3.311	29.222	2.187	3.216	23.082
6	2.162	3.179	32.401	2.101	3.090	26.172
7	1.924	2.829	35.231	1.949	2.867	29.038
8	1.850	2.721	37.952	1.948	2.864	31.902
9	1.572	2.312	40.264	1.869	2.749	34.651
10	1.447	2.129	42.392	1.758	2.585	37.236
11	1.360	1.999	44.392	1.640	2.411	39.647
12	1.326	1.951	46.343	1.569	2.308	41.955
13	1.301	1.914	48.256	1.542	2.267	44.222
14	1.240	1.823	50.080	1.530	2.250	46.472
15	1.183	1.740	51.820	1.526	2.243	48.716
16	1.156	1.700	53.520	1.515	2.228	50.943
17	1.127	1.657	55.177	1.499	2.204	53.147
18	1.104	1.624	56.801	1.473	2.166	55.313
19	1.086	1.597	58.399	1.382	2.033	57.346
20	1.074	1.580	59.979	1.339	1.968	59.314
21	1.059	1.557	61.536	1.200	1.765	61.080
22	1.049	1.543	63.079	1.143	1.681	62.761
23	1.031	1.516	64.595	1.131	1.664	64.424
24	1.009	1.483	66.078	1.125	1.654	66.078
25	.994	1.462	67.540			
26	.981	1.442	68.983			
27	.972	1.429	70.412			
28	.953	1.402	71.814			
29	.937	1.378	73.192			
30	.912	1.341	74.533			
31	.908	1.335	75.867			
32	.891	1.310	77.178			
33	.878	1.291	78.469			
34	.873	1.284	79.753			
35	.861	1.267	81.020			
36	.852	1.253	82.273			
37	.827	1.216	83.488			
38	.806	1.185	84.673			
39	.791	1.163	85.837			
40	.778	1.144	86.981			
41	.771	1.134	88.115			
42	.745	1.096	89.210			

43	.726	1.067	90.277
44	.699	1.028	91.305
45	.682	1.003	92.308
46	.665	.978	93.286
47	.650	.955	94.242
48	.612	.900	95.142
49	.570	.838	95.980
50	.503	.739	96.719
51	.464	.682	97.401
52	.422	.621	98.022
53	.298	.438	98.460
54	.261	.384	98.843
55	.239	.351	99.194
56	.197	.290	99.484
57	.120	.177	99.661
58	.046	.067	99.729
59	.042	.062	99.791
60	.035	.052	99.843
61	.031	.046	99.889
62	.025	.037	99.926
63	.019	.027	99.953
64	.015	.022	99.974
65	.013	.019	99.993
66	.005	.007	100.000
67	.000	.000	100.000
68	.000	.000	100.000

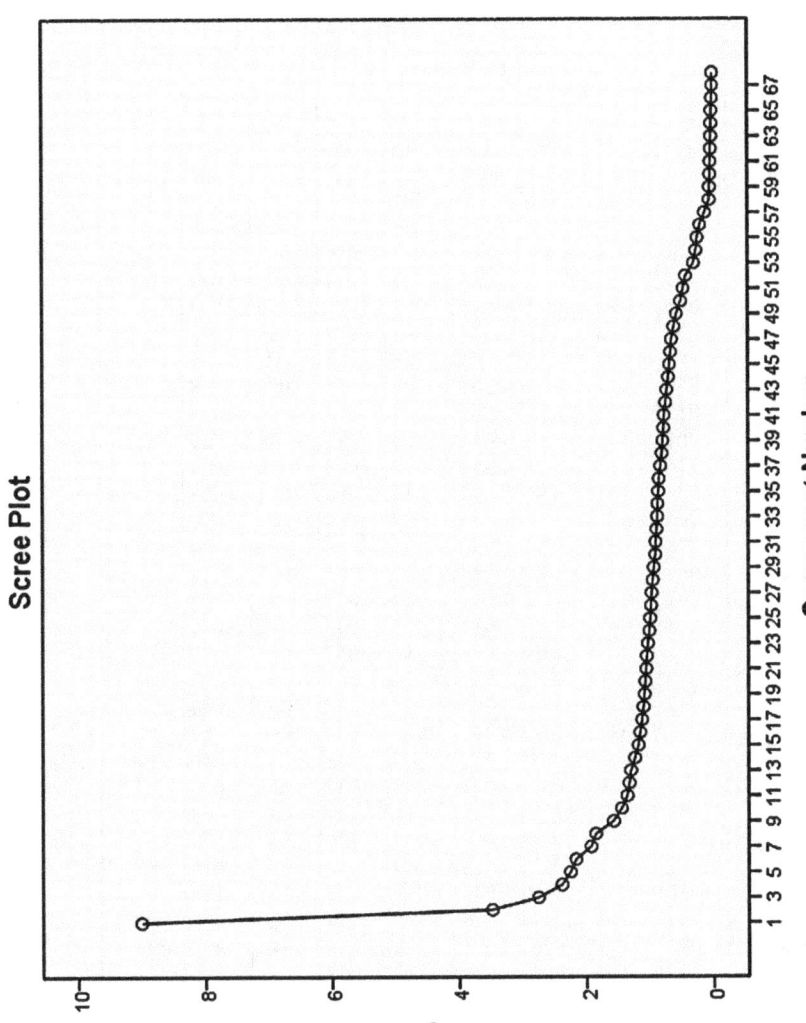

Figure 8: Scree plot

125

Table 32: Factor loadings and Cronbachs Alpha for new constructs

	Component								alpha	
	1	2	3	4	5	6	7	8	old	new
verb	.846	.083	.049	.130	.016	.051	.032	.054	.727	
auxverb	.814	.057	.047	.054	.013	.023	-.022	.001		
present	.777	.041	.051	.190	.031	.040	.043	.079		
funct	.657	.472	.115	.219	.039	.273	.005	.059		
ipron	.654	.031	.043	.142	-.003	.050	.004	-.016		
relativ	.030	.888	.105	.034	-.037	.011	-.016	-.032	.607	
space	.005	.781	.082	.010	-.001	.027	.039	-.024		
prep	.236	.698	.127	.037	.063	.172	.017	.040		
dic	*.498*	*.505*	*.232*	*.188*	*.152*	*.243*	*.091*	*.195*	*remove*	*.782*
article	.369	.443	.097	-.204	.008	.055	.006	.048		
motion	.012	.393	.058	.064	-.077	.038	-.049	-.020		
WC	-.081	-.118	-.935	-.040	-.019	-.019	-.038	-.049	.681	
wps	-.118	-.133	-.929	-.054	-.019	-.035	-.036	-.049		
number	-.174	-.163	-.838	-.065	-.047	-.096	-.047	-.058		
sixltr	*-.206*	*-.032*	*.567*	*-.153*	*.052*	*.033*	*-.017*	*.004*	*remove*	*.807*
ppron	.278	.032	.024	.894	.005	.108	.007	.034	.788	
pronoun	.569	.040	.042	.715	.002	.105	.007	.015		
you	.161	.049	-.002	.680	.029	-.035	.031	.082		
i	.163	-.080	.054	.452	-.015	-.045	-.007	.046		
bio	.031	.003	.052	.011	.954	.035	.088	.029	.711	
health	.020	-.001	.035	-.020	.774	.007	-.079	.023		
ingest	.047	-.011	.036	.046	.532	.057	-.003	.004		
body	-.021	.034	.013	.020	.477	-.004	.306	-.084		
incl	.065	.146	.082	.022	.030	.883	.023	.056	.657	
conj	.180	.091	.057	.064	.038	.734	.018	.060		
cogmech	.263	.087	.121	.115	.027	.534	.007	.062		
we	*.116*	*-.012*	*.019*	*.304*	*-.005*	*.406*	*-.030*	*-.050*	*remove*	*.717*
percept	.030	.004	.053	.012	.049	.012	.912	.015	.683	
see	.058	.032	.046	.004	-.037	.012	.761	.130		
feel	*-.040*	*-.004*	*.031*	*.008*	*.113*	*.024*	*.580*	*-.100*	*remove*	*.734*
posemo	.092	-.006	.076	.051	.008	.044	.046	.892	.892	
affect	.109	.010	.093	.049	.032	.051	.031	.805		
Friend	-.055	-.002	.025	.060	-.006	.063	.009	.367		
excl	.145	.008	.025	.090	-.003	.099	.016	.019	.586	
negate	.243	-.043	.032	.012	.010	-.057	-.014	-.025		.602
tentat	.154	.076	.016	.087	.015	.109	.016	.032		
cause	.186	.005	.054	.035	-.017	.119	-.003	.021	.288	
insight	.104	-.021	.081	.101	.040	.064	-.010	-.036		
adverb	.333	.125	.009	.148	.002	.145	-.021	.018		
anger	.014	.031	.037	.015	-.082	.007	-.018	.050	.612	
death	*-.030*	*.022*	*.035*	*-.018*	*.076*	*-.040*	*-.013*	*-.029*	*remove*	*.752*
negemo	.059	.028	.047	.015	.041	.022	-.012	.095		
hear	.021	-.022	.002	.009	-.024	-.040	.208	-.043	.307	

									alpha
relig	.005	.007	.012	-.028	.004	.015	-.032	-.007	
leisure	-.096	.039	.143	.029	-.024	.038	-.028	.149	.646
sad	.015	.000	.014	-.007	.088	.009	.023	.032	.230
achieve	.018	.107	.060	-.009	-.010	-.043	-.014	.317	
future	.262	.034	.013	.037	-.006	.007	-.013	-.016	.494
discrep	.185	-.005	.015	.158	.010	.054	-.006	.022	
human	.039	.002	.050	-.039	.056	-.015	.021	.043	.385
social	.174	.067	.085	.531	-.002	.123	-.014	.139	
they	.228	.038	-.019	.153	-.028	.053	-.004	-.112	
certain	.096	-.021	.036	.018	-.005	.018	.001	.035	.379
quant	.143	.130	.037	.043	.007	.057	-.004	.074	
work	-.037	.037	.135	-.023	-.027	.018	-.042	-.015	.421
money	.013	.021	.037	.045	-.030	.033	-.032	.118	
past	.299	.096	.008	-.065	-.021	.043	.013	-.013	.314
shehe	-.038	.085	-.004	.207	.011	-.011	.005	.022	
swear	.043	.003	-.005	.033	-.043	-.001	-.003	-.040	.263
sexual	.028	-.031	.026	-.032	.239	.008	-.038	.166	
anx	.040	.030	.016	.001	.051	.016	-.006	.049	
filler	.090	-.111	.012	-.002	.012	.034	.062	.002	.063
time	.048	.431	.053	.014	-.020	-.030	-.035	-.016	
assent	.020	-.031	.036	-.003	-.054	-.002	.045	.086	.121
nonfl	.028	-.009	-.034	.011	.045	.009	-.056	.032	
home	.022	.009	.031	.007	.023	.043	.024	-.019	.102
family	-.038	-.025	.023	.027	-.030	-.008	-.056	.026	
inhib	.036	.036	.036	-.003	.051	.017	-.005	.086	

	Component								alpha	
	9	10	11	12	13	14	15	16	old	new
verb	.116	.132	-.005	-.018	.023	.270	.033	-.005	.727	
auxverb	.129	.031	-.003	-.018	.023	.298	.032	.025		
present	.129	.168	-.031	-.034	-.019	.069	.068	-.006		
funct	.196	.145	.058	-.002	.006	.052	.093	.224		
ipron	.060	.005	-.010	.005	.002	.011	-.006	.149		
relativ	-.001	-.031	-.069	.002	.046	.059	-.041	-.003	.607	
space	-.007	-.087	.045	-.016	-.014	-.011	-.017	.009		
prep	.015	.104	.094	.006	-.039	-.050	.086	.098		
dic	*.139*	*.209*	*.064*	*.110*	*.077*	*.082*	*.141*	*.199*	*remove*	.782
article	-.011	.046	.128	.012	.002	-.039	.080	.110		
motion	-.033	.095	-.228	.019	.070	.101	-.024	-.157		
WC	-.028	-.019	-.025	-.034	-.028	-.003	-.017	-.029	.681	
wps	-.041	-.023	-.025	-.033	-.028	-.007	-.020	-.038		
number	-.053	-.058	-.035	-.051	-.016	-.018	-.045	-.047		
sixltr	*-.078*	*.098*	*-.006*	*.002*	*-.037*	*.018*	*.023*	*-.026*	*remove*	.807
ppron	.077	.028	-.008	-.006	.009	.065	.079	.043	.788	
pronoun	.088	.022	-.011	-.001	.008	.052	.053	.115		
you	.095	.231	.023	-.026	-.011	.257	.055	-.041		
i	.009	.022	-.153	-.005	-.062	-.138	-.341	.049		

127

bio	.008	.003	-.013	-.018	.088	-.001	.040	.007	.711	
health	.003	.038	.082	-.003	-.086	.030	.045	-.024		
ingest	.026	-.031	-.020	.037	.342	-.073	-.101	-.010		
body	-.018	.002	-.063	-.083	.055	.031	.030	.083		
incl	-.072	.024	-.032	.010	-.005	.002	.022	.037	.657	
conj	.263	.274	-.026	-.002	.010	.043	.013	-.022		
cogmech	.282	.502	.008	-.023	-.013	.208	.028	.322		
we	*-.104*	*-.309*	*.058*	*-.008*	*.052*	*.015*	*.097*	*.127*	*remove*	.717
percept	.012	-.001	-.014	.325	.036	-.005	.011	-.004	.683	
see	.016	-.027	.068	-.072	-.153	-.040	-.011	-.060		
feel	*-.020*	*.024*	*-.132*	*-.057*	*.265*	*.035*	*.011*	*.090*	*remove*	.734
posemo	.015	-.008	-.080	.055	.003	-.018	-.025	.126	.892	
affect	.036	-.013	.266	.044	.289	.008	.007	.102		
Friend	-.024	.032	-.055	-.065	-.118	.048	.209	-.109		
excl	.834	.038	.011	-.019	.010	.119	.002	.023	.586	
negate	.666	-.093	-.006	.020	.049	-.050	.027	-.007		.602
tentat	.520	.136	.002	-.035	-.034	.285	.038	.255		
cause	-.026	.691	-.033	-.037	.091	-.077	-.009	-.058	.288	
insight	-.015	.546	.035	-.009	-.046	.113	.038	.216		
adverb	.250	.349	.003	-.013	.018	-.104	.004	.072		
anger	.010	-.025	.754	.015	.145	-.013	.012	-.004	.612	
death	*-.014*	*.020*	*.607*	*-.008*	*-.100*	*.014*	*-.044*	*-.029*	*remove*	.752
negemo	.042	-.014	.583	-.003	.504	.043	.045	-.005		
hear	.025	.005	.028	.791	-.024	.014	.035	-.028	.307	
relig	-.019	-.005	.030	.693	-.049	-.001	-.001	.028		
leisure	-.032	-.067	-.099	.537	.078	-.025	-.048	-.006		.646
sad	.034	-.004	.052	-.042	.775	.033	.013	-.029	.230	
achieve	-.031	.294	-.075	.013	.456	-.011	.004	.078		
future	-.011	-.046	-.009	.012	.024	.747	-.006	.038	.494	
discrep	.200	.069	.014	-.012	.012	.657	-.012	.049		
human	-.003	.028	-.029	-.021	-.022	-.015	.713	.025	.385	
social	.044	.051	.073	.067	.016	.114	.652	.019		
they	.094	-.075	-.065	.015	.079	-.177	.364	.057		
certain	.007	.064	.000	.014	-.017	.107	-.001	.719	.379	
quant	.102	.064	-.031	-.009	.019	-.038	.042	.681		
work	-.041	.187	-.037	-.014	.096	.027	.025	-.037	.421	
money	.051	-.076	-.041	-.039	-.054	.005	-.088	.010		
past	.019	.025	.055	.022	.078	-.012	-.051	-.028	.314	
shehe	.048	-.009	.136	.033	.015	.033	.182	-.041		
swear	.009	.000	.177	.050	.027	-.026	-.045	.011	.263	
sexual	.014	-.011	-.092	.004	-.126	.006	.177	-.046		
anx	.003	.000	.023	.014	.057	.015	.065	.001		
filler	.012	-.005	.051	-.013	-.020	-.020	.058	.035	.063	
time	.027	-.018	-.038	.013	.054	.056	-.031	.074		
assent	-.012	-.094	-.038	-.022	-.004	.009	-.005	.062	.121	
nonfl	.022	.103	.109	.017	-.085	-.012	.020	-.119		
home	-.042	-.051	.031	-.037	-.062	-.013	-.072	.037	.102	

family	-.014	.005	.009	.009	.028	.016	.319	.023	
inhib	.074	.118	.085	-.034	-.090	-.012	-.026	.009	

	Component								alpha	
	17	18	19	20	21	22	23	24	old	new
verb	-.017	.175	.033	.007	.079	.000	.021	.052	.727	
auxverb	-.003	.111	-.003	.007	.044	.019	.017	.030		
present	-.025	-.105	.057	-.005	.046	.006	.019	.060		
funct	.035	.097	-.034	.002	-.018	.001	-.007	-.071		
ipron	-.023	.014	.017	.052	.019	.025	-.053	-.014		
relativ	-.035	.087	.031	.033	.302	.010	.023	.113	.607	
space	.031	-.005	-.016	-.008	-.076	-.018	-.028	-.029		
prep	.106	.039	-.060	-.002	-.112	-.033	-.024	-.053		
dic	*.217*	*.083*	*.022*	*.032*	*.083*	*.010*	*.097*	*.026*	*remove*	*.782*
article	-.016	.077	-.056	-.069	-.114	-.068	-.043	-.126		
motion	-.098	-.018	.133	.120	.072	.024	.075	.229		
WC	-.001	.008	-.019	.007	-.032	-.016	-.021	.010	.681	
wps	-.001	.001	-.016	.007	-.035	-.018	-.020	.012		
number	-.049	-.024	-.013	-.009	-.007	-.015	-.027	.006		
sixltr	*.335*	*.004*	*-.042*	*.061*	*-.032*	*-.058*	*-.009*	*.142*	*remove*	*.807*
ppron	.015	.200	.013	.015	.007	.005	-.019	.029	.788	
pronoun	-.002	.150	.019	.040	.016	.018	-.043	.012		
you	.005	-.297	-.041	-.071	-.019	.000	.100	-.020		
i	-.071	.377	.116	.235	.023	.007	-.021	-.167		
bio	-.050	-.003	.200	.003	-.008	.000	.024	.013	.711	
health	.072	.023	-.073	.133	.033	-.031	-.100	.039		
ingest	-.159	-.127	-.119	-.175	.001	-.039	.202	-.050		
body	-.012	.048	.370	.010	-.071	.108	.010	.057		
incl	.029	.027	.008	.006	-.013	-.010	.016	.017	.657	
conj	.008	-.011	.017	.050	.042	.042	.093	-.079		
cogmech	.046	.021	-.006	.046	.002	-.027	-.013	.186		
we	*.040*	*-.012*	*-.063*	*-.156*	*.065*	*-.018*	*-.252*	*.272*	*remove*	*.717*
percept	-.026	.030	-.009	.001	.023	.038	-.008	.002	.683	
see	-.066	-.049	-.068	-.002	.095	-.198	-.044	-.087		
feel	*.011*	*.037*	*.102*	*-.017*	*-.083*	*.325*	*.065*	*.110*	*remove*	*.734*
posemo	.110	-.038	.012	-.080	-.020	.153	-.012	.093	.892	
affect	.078	-.034	.106	.232	-.015	.117	-.011	.103		
Friend	-.106	.114	-.007	.054	.036	-.129	.061	-.128		
excl	-.016	.001	.011	-.008	.018	.003	-.022	-.015	.586	
negate	.020	.096	.018	-.045	.024	.010	-.025	.214		.602
tentat	.006	-.048	-.019	.125	-.016	-.022	-.028	-.179		
cause	.055	-.075	.004	-.082	-.003	-.030	-.002	.195	.288	
insight	.087	.096	-.018	.065	-.036	-.003	-.088	-.051		
adverb	-.095	-.043	.016	.037	.228	.195	.089	-.089		
anger	-.044	-.029	.319	.160	.001	-.005	.028	.082	.612	
death	*-.044*	*.176*	*-.125*	*-.103*	*.037*	*.052*	*.015*	*.017*	*remove*	*.752*
negemo	-.032	-.001	.170	.525	.007	-.019	-.002	.039		

hear	.035	.096	-.027	.034	.011	-.006	-.045	.001	.307	
relig	.006	.020	.044	.044	-.026	.002	-.088	.008		
leisure	-.147	-.114	.020	-.123	.022	-.016	.228	-.068		.646
sad	.010	.073	-.042	.124	.023	-.048	-.028	-.116	.230	
achieve	.258	.049	-.059	-.198	-.038	-.073	-.171	.143		
future	.019	.004	-.010	-.016	.031	.014	-.009	.039	.494	
discrep	.014	-.006	-.006	.039	-.026	-.014	.000	-.039		
human	-.080	.042	.076	.062	.032	.020	-.001	-.075	.385	
social	.018	.117	.015	-.056	.007	-.018	.087	.048		
they	.172	-.065	-.006	.123	.020	.014	-.016	.095		
certain	-.052	.041	.025	-.017	.102	.012	.047	.118	.379	
quant	.025	-.104	-.031	.012	-.017	-.035	.007	-.119		
work	.743	.027	-.017	-.065	-.013	-.037	-.075	.016	.421	
money	.691	-.102	.008	.027	.043	.016	.230	-.055		
past	-.005	.651	-.025	.028	.089	-.024	.014	-.013	.314	
shehe	-.049	.620	.019	-.095	-.053	.012	.050	.002		
swear	.025	-.052	.751	-.058	.006	-.013	.005	-.024	.263	
sexual	-.050	.076	.592	-.003	.015	-.056	-.070	-.052		
anx	-.023	-.036	-.080	.798	-.018	-.002	.000	.093		
filler	.048	-.053	.001	-.018	.693	-.026	-.043	-.075	.063	
time	-.048	.170	.002	.000	.659	.024	.024	.088		
assent	-.047	.026	.050	.006	-.082	.672	-.006	.067	.121	
nonfl	.026	-.042	-.117	-.007	.101	.629	-.055	-.161		
home	.165	-.055	-.035	.019	-.025	-.055	.721	.028	.102	
family	-.086	.250	-.011	-.034	-.006	.010	.495	.042		
inhib	-.011	-.018	-.054	.108	-.041	-.055	.045	.718		

Table 33: Results of models 40 - 42

Variable	Model 40 Views	Model 41 Diggs	Model 42 Comments
Intercept	25426.081 (2341.481)***	1736.622 (120.411)***	292.885 (22.194)***
Ratio of net. diggs after 2h	-25786.847 (2617.155)***	-1480.901 (134.588)***	-286.342 (24.808)***
Topic			
Gaming	-320.591 (2745.047)	-98.145 (141.165)	-7.487 (26.020)
Lifestyle	-543.823 (1901.994)	-82.463 (97.810)	-5.385 (18.029)
Offbeat	6668.082 (1911.768)**	173.872 (98.313)	15.237 (18.121)
Science	-3540.470 (1953.383)	-192.947 (100.453)	-36.834 (18.516)*
Sports	-3836.294 (2458.468)	-324.423 (126.427)*	-37.541 (23.303)
Technology	-2219.004 (1859.906)	-147.414 (95.646)	-21.041 (17.630)
World & Business	-1007.286 (2002.273)	91.113 (102.967)	123.093 (18.979)***
Media			
Images	-5873.636 (1658.066)***	-363.607 (85.266)***	-36.333 (15.716)*
News	13079.018 (1980.242)***	346.125 (101.834)**	-17.922 (18.770)
Adjusted R square	.323	.265	.247

* $p < .05$, ** $p < .01$, *** $p < .001$

Note—The reference category for Topic is entertainment. for Media it is video

**Marketing im globalen Wettbewerb
Marketing & Global Competition**

Herausgegeben von / Edited by Oliver P. Heil

Band / Vol. 1   Daniel Langer / Oliver P. Heil: Luxury: Marketing & Management. Tools and Strategies to Manage Luxury Products in a Profitable and Sustainable Fashion. Comprehensive Model of Luxury Management and New Scientific Insights Based on New Concepts and Empirical Evidence for Luxury Managers and Sophisticated Luxury Consumers. 2011.

Band / Vol. 2   Mark Elsner: Information Propagation on the Web 2.0. Two Essays on the Propagation of User-Generated Content and How It Is Affected by Social Networks. 2012.

www.peterlang.de